CW01663813

The MAGIC of HR

The MAGIC of HR

Principles to Grow Your Business Like a People Pro

Claire Ward

authors
AND CO.

First published in Great Britain in 2023
by Authors & Co.
www.authorsandco.pub

ISBN 978-1-915771-28-5 (paperback)
ISBN 978-1-915771-29-2 (hardback)

Contents

1
People-Smart

Want a happy team? Want a team which goes the extra mile? Want a team which brings you suggestions not objections? These all become possible when you get your baseline principles right. *The MAGIC of HR* is for those who don't really 'do' HR and People but want to get the best from their team.

From org chart to people-smart

When you started your own business, you probably envisioned the perfect organisation chart, whether you sketched it on a napkin, a business plan, or an investor deck. You imagined each role fitting neatly into place, each person bringing the skills and expertise you needed to your venture. With the right people on board, progress would be swift and before you knew it you'd be collecting awards for the Fastest Growing Business in history. Hurrah!

But let's face it, real life isn't always so neat and tidy once the people actually arrive...

People are undoubtedly crucial to your business growth plans, but beyond the creation of an org chart, they often take a back seat to your marketing or sales efforts in the early stages.

Sometimes business owners think they're not *BIG* enough to have HR and People plans. Sometimes they simply don't know what they don't know. However, sometimes they don't realise the tremendous boost doing this right can bring to their business.

That is where this book comes in: I help you stay ahead of the game, and ensure you have the knowledge to make your team thrive and identify the key areas that will deliver the most value for your investment. I guide you through the principles of a simple HR and People framework – *the MAGIC framework* – offering real-life examples and insights to help you build and retain a brilliant team that supports your growth.

The phrase 'people are your greatest asset' holds a special truth. They bring the ideas, energy, support and delivery you need to build your dreams. But sometimes – *if you do not intentionally create the right environment* – they can also become your greatest liability.

You may think the biggest liability in an employment sense is the risk of legal action in an employment tribunal. After all, countless services out there offer insurance and scare tactics to protect against potential employee actions.

However, my years of experience have shown that these risks tend to be outliers and are *not* the greatest threats to business owners.

On the contrary, the biggest derailments of even the best business models that suck the life out of otherwise energised leaders relate to teams not reaching their potential. Instead of ideas and contributions, you end up with the 'noise' that arises when teams aren't engaged, or worse, when they actively impede progress.

Early doors in your business, you have very little idea how much time you will have to spend on the 'people' aspects of your business and the medley of issues they can present you with. I don't only mean the practicalities of hiring and payroll. I am referring to the time you spend bringing your plans to life, addressing concerns raised by your team, and managing your own confusion or frustration when they do not perform as expected. Hours and hours can be consumed in debates about team members' concerns or through lack of alignment and communication hiccups, all of which leave you feeling drained.

These challenges are hard to quantify. Individually, they aren't always difficult to address, but when you're handling them alone, they can become a drag. Not only do they impact the success of your business, they also diminish your enjoyment of your role. After all, it's unlikely you started your business with these kinds of images on your vision board.

Hundreds and thousands of businesses continue to employ people on a daily basis in a very satisfactory manner without receiving complaints and without anticipating any legal risks on the horizon in this regard. However, many of them fail to realise their full potential or move forward as they could. What if you want more than a risk-free environment? What if you want to exceed mere satisfaction? *What if you want to fly?*

For this, you need to get people-smart.

You need a sprinkling of MAGIC...

The MAGIC principles in this book are accessible to everyone running a business and will give you the opportunity to realise the potential of having an awesome team. Perhaps you have some idea of what HR and People can do for you, but you may be limiting your practice of it to processes and compliance, and ignoring the elephant in the room: the opportunity for growth in a friction-free way. You won't find a whole tonne of employment law in this average-sized tome, therefore. There certainly won't be any prescribing about policies and processes. You will get a simple framework that shows you how to design what you want within your team to ensure that your business and people prosper, rather than just exist.

You're welcome

Years ago, I was hired for a period to act as the HR Director of a growing business that employed about sixty people. To be perfectly frank, they didn't know what they wanted from me. Someone had told them that, given their plans to go *big*, it might be useful to 'get someone involved who knew something on the people-side of things'. I ummed and ahhed about it as I wasn't quite sure of their beliefs, but was persuaded it was the right thing to do and so I signed on the dotted line.

My introduction to the business was not as ideal as it could have been: whilst people were nice to me, I was tolerated rather than welcomed by certain members of the leadership team and it was very clear that some felt I was merely there to sort out the holiday rota. Despite this tepid reception, as I've always liked being able to show how to add value in the kind of environment which seems to welcome it least, I knuckled down and got to work.

There had been a flurry of leavers before I joined and in my early conversations with remaining team members many shared their cynicism that anything would be learnt from these departures. Despite this, I set about looking at what would make the biggest difference to the team in terms of their contribution and engagement within the business. I soon put in place upgrades to their strategy in development, communications and support as well as recruitment, onboarding and some of their other more operational processes.

I even found time to sort out the holiday rota...

Fast forward six months to when it was time for me to leave, the HR and People function in the team looked noticeably different from when I'd started: I had set up two new offices, increased the headcount by 20 percent and worked to stabilise the existing team. But the difference was seen not just in terms of the 'hard' data. The general 'vibe' had changed too. There was a greater sense of openness among the team, and people seemed more collegiate and less inclined to challenge every decision that was communicated to them. Better still, the company numbers were heading in the right direction.

It was not all down to me, obviously, but as I was leaving, the CEO pulled me aside and thanked me. "What for?" I asked, keen to practise my specific-feedback-is-best skills. They answered, "For showing me what HR can actually 'do' for a business."

Inside my mind at the time, my hands were clasped and I was bowing with a short, "You're welcome." On the outside I settled for a brief but genuine thanks. As I walked away I realised that like so many other businesses, this one was initially so focused on the policies and processes they felt they needed that they almost missed the opportunity of thinking about **how** they treated their teams and the benefits this brought them.

Do you believe in MAGIC?

The last twenty-five years have given me the opportunity to work with over three hundred companies across multiple industries around the world. I have observed and had access to the factors which have influenced the success (or failure in some cases) of those businesses. I have been allowed to see the hits, the misses and the maybes when it comes to the business of their people. And I've distilled this insight down into five key principles that I believe have the greatest impact on the success of your teams.

When your team are flowing; when they are all working together in harmony; when they are brimming with ideas; when they all get along and contribute without the need for you to step in at every stage; when their motivation is high and they often go 'above and beyond' what you've asked; when they are productive and step in to help everyone else on their team get the job done – this is the state that I call 'MAGIC'.

MAGIC is more than just a feeling you get, however. It is more than just a state of being:

- **M**eaning
- **A**ccountability
- **G**rowth
- **I**nclusion
- **C**are

These are the principles I am going to explore with you in this book: explaining the meaning, the importance and (crucially) the ways in which you can bring these to life in your own business. It is possible to create some MAGIC of your very own– whether you're two people in a room or twenty people looking for more.

For some, this may be a brush up on some old tactics or a chance to supplement existing practices with some new ideas. Others may find confirmation that they are on the right track. Whichever stage you are at with your business,

I guarantee you will learn something you can implement from the next few pages.

You want to grow. Your team wants to grow. Everyone wants some sort of growth: it's inherent in all of us. But regardless of your specific growth plans for your business – organic or acquisition/investment – your people are going to be the accelerant for these. I'm going to take you through the principles that can give you the edge and help you light the spark. You are already on the right track by getting this far: picking up this book shows that you want to do the 'right thing' with your team and care about their success and contribution.

You might think that setting them up with their laptop, a job description and faith that you will give them all the autonomy in the world to be successful would do the trick; however, in many cases people need more than this. They need to be given a framework to thrive.

This book will give you a framework to help you do just that: it will simplify your people strategy by helping you understand why people 'do what they do' and what elements you need to have in place and to maximise their impact.

The good news is that creating some MAGIC in your team is not about money or heavy time investments. Nor is it about having an MBA or your very own CIPD qualification. Time and again I see people who achieve amazing results through their people when they start with a positive intent and some core principles to work by. No-one is born an HR and People expert, after all, but nor do you need to apply to become one.

MAGIC secrets

I have spent the best part of my career advising people how to create this MAGIC in their teams: how to hire, manage and grow their teams with their strategy, their operation and their scenario planning. I have worked within the large corporate space, run my own businesses and advised countless startups and growing SMEs about their HR and People, all with great success. Sometimes this success has been in the sense of day-to-day operational process and management. Many times it has also been in the thorny *how-the-hell-do-I-get-out-of-this-situation?* sense of management. Other times, I have been faced with a *what-do-they-think-this-is?-A-holiday-camp?* situation.

I have worked with businesses which employ two staff or two thousand. I have discovered that, regardless of the industry you are in, the common denominators for success with your people remain the same.

This book is about the secret principles of the HR and People strategy which have carried various companies into the big leagues. Many of the companies I have worked with over the years have gone on to be acquired, to grow or even to IPO. So if you're a business owner or leader who – *like me* – is a little impatient, more than a little ambitious and likes working smarter to get results from your team, read on.

Many of the insights I share are evidence-based, either through my own experience or externally referenced studies, and I have no shame in summarising the areas I believe have the most impact on your people. I don't like wading through copious amounts of text to get the nuggets, so I don't see why you should either.

However, I fully believe in arming yourself with as much information as possible. Whilst some of the suggestions I make in this book may feel uncomfortable, I ask that in the same way you picked up this book to learn something you didn't know, you keep your mind open to different ways of adapting your own style. There is no single track that will translate into every organisation as a template, but there are common denominators of how your employees will experience your business: that is the system we refer to.

If you're thinking about how your team can work better together, do more for you and cause less grief, this is the framework for you. If you want to find out how to sprinkle a bit of MAGIC dust, read on...

2

Good news, friends! Anyone can create MAGIC in their teams

Sam runs a technology business in the heart of the City of London. It's not huge, their software doesn't focus on a 'sexy' industry and I'm not sure you'll have read about them in the press. But we've been working with Sam over the last few years and have seen the company go from strength to strength with their sales, increasing their head-count several times over, and building each year on the success of the previous one, all without fanfare. They're a pleasure to work with as a partner and their data reflects this internally too: they experience double the retention rates of other companies in their industry with strong engagement scores every time they're surveyed and boast glowing reviews online from their customers and team alike.

Despite their success, they're also not flush with spare cash as they plough what they can back into the business as investment. They're not going on any spending spree with the team members in the process: no sky-high salaries or huge bonuses being dished out to keep people happy. In fact, I think their budget line for HR and People in the first year we worked with them would have been the equivalent of a long lunch for two in any typical London restaurant. Nevertheless, that hasn't stopped them from building out a great team and a great business.

When Sam started the business, she didn't want it to run in the same way as the businesses she had previously worked in. Sure, she might have 're-purposed' the employment contracts and a couple of policies from her previous firm, but that's as far as the carryover went. And in terms of how she wanted people to feel when working with her, even when she took on her first two employees, she knew she wanted to create a different place from the very beginning and that 'how' they were going to work would be a key element to keep in mind as they grew. She believed that people *weren't* out to screw their employers at the first opportunity and that they *wanted* to contribute wherever they could. In everything she did, she kept this in mind, even when there were just two of them in a room.

The budgets may have been low initially, but the company has a strong desire for the best for everyone and the team understands this, translating into mutual respect and everyone doing right by each other. It was never about the money. Every year they plan out what they need *from* and *for* their people and every year they get in early to share what their team can expect in terms of training, well-being and support to help them do this. It's a two-way conversation in which they listen to what people say as they join and grow. Whilst no company is perfect, as a consequence of this intention and by embodying the spirit of everything I write about within the MAGIC framework, few (if any) employee relations issues have reared their heads as they have grown from two to ten and now to over fifty people. The effort and dedication people put into the team's success is considerably higher than in most teams I've seen.

Design thinking

When you want to inject a bit of MAGIC, it's never too early to design how you see your team.

When you have three people in your business, it can feel a little nonsensical to consider what the team will look and feel like at fifty or one hundred people. But if you're serious about growth, there may only be a few months or years between these stages. Moreover, if you don't intentionally think about how to design your team and what you want from them, it's more likely that circumstances will dictate how they become rather than the other way around. You may feel that your team of three people works fine right now, but what works with three will not work in quite the same way with fifty and will definitely not work with one hundred!

Your intentions around your people are important at every stage.

In one of my first HR roles, I was employee number eight. My boss, the HR Director, was employee number five.

There were four founders of this business. Such was their recognition that the team culture, structure and overall people function would be key ingredients to achieving what they wanted that they went big and went early with the HR and People team. It was with a considerable effort that this plan paid off and we hit all growth targets for the first eighteen months. By then we were an HR team of six in a business of 190. It would have been almost impossible to pull that off without the planning which had taken place in advance. It would have been nigh-on impractical to retrospectively fit the core principles around that.

For other businesses, however, the initial growth plans might not be as accelerated as that. Therefore, whilst the intentions are there, the action is somewhat scaled back. Consider the organically grown business of forty people I worked with for a few years who were starting to think about expansion and growth and tentatively having conversations with external parties about helping them achieve this. They wanted to have the foundations in place and do the 'right thing' by their team and any future investors. I worked with them to ensure that some fundamental principles of responsibility, support and focus were in place and surrounded by the right processes.

After a while, the investors started to knock on their door. One of them asked to sit down with me to discuss what the HR and People function looked like: they were keen to understand more about what they might be getting into. They were impressed when I explained how the teams operated, how we encouraged accountability in the teams and how we also looked to measure the impact. They said,

"I wouldn't have expected to see this level of maturity in a business of this size." The investment was duly made and although this won't have been the sole reason for it, I'm sure it was a contributing factor.

Conversely, I've seen companies which seem to be flying on the outside. They have achieved investment, have column inches about them everywhere, have a publicly-known CEO - yet on the inside, things aren't so great.

One such company expanded very quickly and, in addition to their scale of growth, were extremely proud of the collective 'smartness' of their team, not to mention how many of their team had MBAs, PHDs and any other group of letters you could imagine after their names. They thought of themselves as extremely tech savvy and cutting edge and there was a budget for pretty much any tool you wanted to use across the business. The team were encouraged to be collaborative and there were endless suggestions of HR and People practices which team members had seen used or written about in their Silicon Valley icons.

All of this would have been good, yet you only had to scratch the surface of this extremely well-constructed image, and the veneer started to peel away. It is true that collaboration was possible in their processes on a technical level and it's likely true that the majority of the individuals in their teams were more than capable of contributing. They were definitely bright. However, putting them all together in an environment obsessed with being 'smarter' than others and without any real thought for how the team should look, function and feel, revealed a business which was frankly devoid of soul.

Such was the obsession with moving faster and faster, that projects were ill-considered and the collaboration they so desperately wanted fell apart in the disorganisation. No-one seemed to have a plan, save for borrowing from everyone else. And whilst I'm all for 'borrowed brilliance' when you use a practice that's worked before, even those need consideration to integrate it with your own culture. The output of this in financial terms was an extremely costly turnover of their team that crippled the business and the loss of the collective intelligence they had sought to use to bolster their credibility. No-one stayed because everyone knew that in that business no-one really – *at heart* – gave a damn about them.

It's easier to avoid this if you start early and design with the best of intentions therefore. Whilst there's never a 'right stage' to start doing this, a bit like investing, the best time to start is now!

Your 'ideal' team

One of the things you might have done to date is imagine your ideal client or customer: you have worked out what their needs are, tried to understand what motivates them and what sort of product or service will help them. Most of you will be very comfortable doing this kind of exercise, but I doubt that many of you have spent a fraction of the time thinking about your 'ideal employee'.

You know your ideal customer will find just the right support, product or service from you and your business to drive their growth because that's what you have spent so much time designing and planning. It is core to your success. *But what about your ideal team?* What kind of outputs do you want them to deliver? What behaviours do you want them to exhibit? And what support and environment do they each *need* in order to contribute to your growth?

Unlike the process of looking at your ideal client, when you design your ideal employee you aren't concerned about their demographics. *Their age, online shopping preferences and number of kids, for example, are distinctly* not *the kind of data that has any place here*. Instead, you focus on the ideal psychographics you want to see: the behaviours and the communication styles; the personality types which will thrive in your ideal company.

Take a moment to imagine what your dream team would look like: what traits would you like to see in them, your stellar cast or your All-Stars?

Use the following questions to prompt your thoughts:

- How do you want them to do their jobs?
- What behaviours do you want to show up when they interact with your clients and colleagues?
- How do you want them to contribute?
- How do you want them to feel about their jobs? Their colleagues? Your business?

- What do you want them to say when you're not there?

Do the questions help you capture any recurring themes? The chances are that your answers include some of the following: you want them to be comfortable enough to get on with their jobs without you micromanaging them; you want them to be self-motivated and focused on the task in hand without needing constant oversight; you want them to use their own initiative and look out for things which might need doing or changing in the business; you want them to solve problems when they arise without needing to check with you every step of the way; you want them to support their team members *(and you)* by helping out whenever there's a need; you want them to enjoy their job and bring you solutions and not complaints...

All of these are entirely possible if you believe that they can do this and you're willing to put in the effort to make it happen.

Abracadabra! Let's make MAGIC.

3
Meaning

My first ever interview in HR was a bit of a long shot if I'm honest. The company was new, had deep pockets and big plans. I left the interview buzzing and went home to my husband waxing lyrical about how amazing the opportunity was. It didn't matter that I knew sweet nothing about IT beyond switching on my own computer or that the commute across London would be a mammoth slog. I felt such a strong connection with them that I would have taken any job they offered.

What mattered to me and what piqued my interest was how they spoke about the customers, what a difference the company had made (and could continue to make) to them and the fact that my role would be a key part of doing this. The 'sell' had been on what my role would be and its contribution to the wider group. Helping others and having a sense of achievement had always been important to me and so it was a no-brainer to sign my job offer when it arrived.

I was ready to roll up my sleeves and get stuck in. And boy, did I get stuck in.

For the next two years, I worked my socks off. We built the team and expanded the company rapidly. It was the first time I'd found a job where I felt a meaningful spark of magic, which in turn fuelled my motivation and ultimately success during that time. What's more, everyone else around me seemed to feel the same. Time flew by so quickly and despite there being some hefty hours put in, I loved every minute of it.

Reflecting on what made it such a special place to work, one thing stood out: at every point in my tenure, I understood what the business stood for and was clear on the part I played and why it mattered.

Even after I exited *(in that particular business I wrote my own redundancy letter, which is perhaps a story for a different chapter in a very different book!)* I still had great respect for them. It wasn't **just** the growth that I believed in - although from business, to copy, to recruitment, I know that growth sells - but what they were trying to do felt significant to me.

Meaning matters

Since then, as I've built my career out, I've spent hundreds of hours interviewing hundreds of people for various jobs in mostly startup and growth environments. Regardless of the role they were seeking or the company they were applying for, the common denominator was that they were all interested in those companies that made them feel they could be 'part of something'.

Great pay and location were good. It was even better if they felt they could get along with their potential team members. But as with my own example, all those factors seemed quite transactional and not the overriding draw when it came to offers. On the contrary, a driving force behind their decision-making appeared to be how they felt about the business on an emotional level: why it existed, who it served and what values it held in its pursuit of all of these. Ultimately, how they **felt** about it and what it represented to them were what mattered.

I was taught in my early years that giving people good 'pay and rations' will satisfy people, but most people I interviewed were not saying, "I want a job that pays well," they were saying, "I want a job that matters." (Ideally, they wanted to be paid well too, of course.)

My experience of the importance of meaning in creating the magic in teams and in using it for growing your business is backed up by a 2020 McKinsey & Company survey [1] which showed 82 percent of employees believe it is important that their company has a purpose and that their work has meaning and also by PWC's study in 2016 [2] which found that millennials who have a strong connection to the purpose of their organisation are 5.3 times more likely to stay.

A person can find meaning in what their company believes in and its overall purpose just as much as in their day-to-day work and interactions. When a company cares about more than just making money, it shows. And when it shows clearly, it becomes a magnet for those who want to align with the same things.

As it turns out, drilling down into what that 'something' means to people at work is a deeper question which varies according to every person you ask, but one thing is for sure: most of us are realists and recognise that we won't all find a cure for cancer or save lives in the literal sense of the word. The 'something' we look for in this regard, therefore, doesn't need to affect millions, but we do need to feel pride in it because that gives us greater fulfilment.

And since we spend an estimated 30 percent of our whole lives at work, who wouldn't want to make that time matter?

Think about those moments at a party when someone asks, "So, what do you do?" Everyone wants to respond with excitement and positivity to this question. They want to talk about how their work contributes to their field of expertise, makes the world a better place in some way or helps others.

This desire to make a difference through what we do with our lives and the choices we make isn't new: we've always wanted it, in both our personal relationships and in our families. We now more than ever however, also seek fulfilment through our jobs.

Manifesting your team

For the whole of my working career at least, employers have been in some sort of 'war for talent' and hiring has never been a walk in the park. But since the time I donned my first Jigsaw suit *(remember wearing suits?)* and lined up my clipboard ready to start my first interviews, the workforce has become pickier than ever as the choice of opportunities has swelled.

A current search yields nearly 1.25 million jobs available (ONS [3]) in the UK alone. With some of the lowest national unemployment figures in the whole of my lifetime, even as we teeter on the edge of a recession in 2023, the recruitment challenges have been well documented and competition for hiring of your roles is rife. People vote with their feet and when it comes to hiring, they want to work with people and businesses who care about the same kind of things as they do. Standing up and standing tall about what kind of business you are will help you stand out in this crowd.

In practice, this means working at making your business resonate more than the next one they see. Focus on what's important to your company and then shout about it loudly!

The benefits of having meaning in your business keep on coming beyond your recruitment efforts. Providing meaningful work for everyone helps make work far more enjoyable and engaging. Essentially, past this initial stage, it becomes even more important that people understand the purpose of their jobs and the company they're representing. Without it, the glue that keeps them with you can wear off.

When someone feels that their work matters, when they take pride in what they do and really care about it, they are much more likely to put in extra discretionary effort to make sure things are as good as they can be. Ultimately this leads to a working environment where quality, dedication and commitment show up as a happier team, customers and investors.

Say goodbye to feeling like you've got to crack the whip the whole time and that it's 'all on you', and hello to your team going the extra mile and making sure that everything is covered.

It's not just HR and People-speak either. Even without the vast amount of research on employee engagement available just a short online search away, you know that you've been miserable working in certain roles and tasks compared with others. You also know that when you've felt the connection in what you're doing and have felt like your work has mattered, you're far more likely to have stayed that extra hour or two to see a project through or thought that little bit more about how to solve a problem or raised your hand to help your team out.

I've been privileged to work with amazing businesses that have a significant and sometimes high-profile positive impact on people's lives, from climate change to dementia care and research through to those which provide life skills for disadvantaged people. These businesses have a clear purpose for existing which is recognisable to most people.

It might seem easier for a business with a more obvious positive impact like this to create meaning for the work their teams have than it is for you. After all, they can highlight all the benefits of their products and services in a way that everyone understands 'does good' and plaster this all over their website,adverts, other recruitment and marketing materials.

But whilst they may have some advantage in this regard, the multitude of other businesses in the UK who aren't charities, health care providers or 'green' businesses are not precluded from being able to show that they have meaning and value too.

As I've alluded to above, what matters to people is a deeply personal thing: indeed, one person's interest in studying data will be another person's insomnia cure. And whilst I personally might find pride in seeing someone's confidence blossom as I help them solve a problem relating to how to get two people's derailed working relationship back on track, many other people would switch off immediately when presented with that situation and would much rather spend their time writing code, trading NFTs or planning parties.

You do not need to know everybody inside out and know that all their hopes, dreams and fears match your own in order to build a successful team. What you need to do is clarify what matters to you and then put it out there clearly and regularly to others so that you attract the people who instinctively align with those.

In essence, it is like manifesting your team.

By taking this approach, instead of simply hoping for the right people to come along and join your team, you are actively seeking out those who share your understanding and interest in the world and who can contribute to what you are building.

Forty-two

Unless you've been living under a rock, you will no doubt have heard of Simon Sinek. His *Find Your Why* TED talk and subsequent YouTube videos are some of the most viewed in the world. If you haven't seen them, please search online in your next tea break.

In his work over the past ten years, Sinek has communicated some great ideas about individuals or businesses having a purpose and how organisations use this purpose as the centre of their messaging and marketing. His ideas have given many people food for thought about their own aims and inspired them to think about how these can accelerate their impact on the market.

But it's also the kind of work which has put the fear of God into many. In the same way that I've seen people tie themselves in knots during reflection time on corporate away days, the idea of clarifying 'why' your business exists can seem such an insurmountable question that it causes panic as you disappear into yourself trying to answer it.

One of my favourite books growing up was *The Hitchhiker's Guide to the Galaxy* by Douglas Adams. In it, the supercomputer (known as Deep Thought) was asked, "*What is the meaning of life?*" It dutifully crunched all the data it had on the world and the people in it and after a long while, it summarised this abundance of data in one very neat answer: forty-two!

Whilst this was a fictional creation, I still love the idea of boiling something seemingly so vast down to a simple output. The good news is that the purpose of your business *can* be reasonably simple and straightforward to surface. Not perhaps as straightforward as Deep Thought found the meaning of life to be, but certainly nothing to scare you.

Even in the business world, you don't need to over-complicate it. Of course, the answer to *What is the meaning behind my company?* is never going to be binary. But you aren't looking at what gives meaning to the whole world or the complex variabilities of a mass of the population. The only place you need to start when clarifying the meaning of your business is with yourself.

You might already be very clear on what matters to you and how you do business or what direction you want it to take. Many people find this self-evident, even if they haven't articulated it or written it down. But if you're not so clear on the meaning of your business or haven't jotted it somewhere, then you might want to have a reflection point here and grab a pencil...

Start by thinking about what your business stands for.

As commercial as you are, it's unlikely that you set up your business solely to make money. It is much more likely you had a belief of some sort in mind and the effect that this could have on others: your customers, readers, whoever the people are that your business serves.

For every household mission statement (think Tesla's *'To accelerate the world's transition to sustainable energy'*), there are equally effective and valid statements as simple as *'to be there for our customers providing the best advice in SW1'*. Perhaps the latter isn't as inspirational as Tesla's, however, the main thing is that you know what you want to be known for, what feels right to you and that it conveys what you are genuinely focused on achieving.

The purpose of my own business, The HR Hub, is to help business owners create employee magic within their teams. We do this by ensuring that our clients have peace of mind and are prepared for what comes next, in whatever form that takes and in a way which is individual to them. For some this means growing their business and fulfilling their plans knowing that they are compliant with employment law at a basic level. For others it's being prepared for a difficult conversation with one of their team or having a clear strategy to accelerate their people structure that we've worked with them to create. None of these may change the world itself, but it may change *their* world.

I also care about having fun in the way we work, being as supportive as we can to our clients, keeping things as simple as possible and being nice to others, an underrated but extremely important aspect of work to me and to the rest of the team. These are essentially all the things I like and which matter to me in my life and I want to show them in the work we do.

In your world, it may be the quality of your products, the innovation of what you are doing, the specific technology you work with or just providing a damn good service that's needed. All these things can be communicated to your team and people in a way which lights a spark in them. Remember, you're not looking to copy others and what they've done. You're looking to be as authentic as possible to attract others who care about the same things.

You might articulate the meaning of your business with a vision or mission statement that sums it all up in an inspirational and impactful way to your team. Others skip the creation of a statement but are clear on the kind of things they want to happen in the next few years by creating long-term goals and outlining their direction. Others satisfy themselves by simply understanding their customers and how they can help them and by communicating this.

So don't beat yourself with the lingo. Just ask yourself a few simple questions:

1. *What's important to you?*
2. *Why do you do what you do (beyond making money)?*
3. *What impact do you want to have on those around you?*
4. *Why did you start the business?*

5. *What sort of things do you want people to say about you when you're not in the room?*
6. *What do you want to be known for?*
7. *Who do you want to help?*
8. *What kind of behaviours do you want to see in people you do business with?*

Listing the answers to these will start to unearth what matters to **you.**

Years ago, a macabre but nonetheless valid alternative process to uncovering the meaning you have was shared with me: imagine your funeral and someone is delivering your eulogy. Do you want it to be along the lines of, *"Here lies Dave Taylor, he nailed every supplier for everything they had..."* or, *"Here lies Dave Taylor, my God, he cared about those around him..."*?

I have worked in companies where the integrity of the owner shone through and made anyone who worked there full of pride. Conversely, I've worked within teams where the opposite is true.

In one such business, they did all the 'right' things you would expect in terms of setting out their values and what they stood for. They conducted exercises to get people to input ideas, held workshops and then plastered the walls with pictures that represented their values and the behaviours they wanted to see. But it was clear to anyone who worked with them for more than a week, that what mattered most (and was in fact the *only* thing that mattered) was money. They did not even pretend to take pride in what they did or that it benefitted the customers they served. In fact, if anything, they took pride in screwing over their customers whenever they could, something even their customers instinctively seemed to know and dislike them for. People saw through this straight away.

It was a god-awful place to work for many reasons. I hired some extremely talented people during my tenure with them, lured in by the glitzy office and shiny client list, but whilst some ended up staying for a reasonable time *(everyone has to eat!)* my work just turned into a never-ending stream of negotiations with retention bonuses that cost the business a fortune and didn't do a single thing to increase the engagement of the team. Everyone knew it was all BS. They strung it out as long as they could but still left. After a while, even golden handcuffs go rusty...

There is no 'right' way to do this, but what's important in creating the magic in your team, whichever way you go, is to stand for **something**.

From the horse's mouth

People aren't mind readers. Once you are clear in your own mind what you stand for and what it means to work for you, the next key part is to share it with others and point them in the right direction.

Struggling for inspiration? Everyone loves a good story, so start by sharing with your team one important moment in your business that meant a lot to you or prompted you to start the business in the first place. You can start this at interview time and then build on it with questions to start to uncover what matters to them:

When did you first start to love what you do? What difference have you made to someone's life? What interesting people have you met along the way? What is the most rewarding thing you've done recently?

Better still, if you can, ask those in receipt of the benefits of your business to come along and share these with your team.

Various businesses I've worked in have had a couple of clients come in and talk to the team at company-wide meetings about the value they get from the service or product provided. However good your own presentation skills are, it's always more impactful to hear it from the horse's mouth.

Daily dose of meaning

Meaning for people however, is also however realised as much from their day-to-day experiences as it is from a company's vision or purpose.

After all, it's not typical or natural for your team to start each day reminding themselves of their company's overall mission statement. But understanding how their tasks will contribute to the wider plans, how they can impact others and how they can influence them with everything they do on a regular basis, will give them a daily dose of meaning that reinforces their significance.

There is a well-trotted-out story about a man who swept the floors at NASA. He was once asked what his job was and he responded, "Helping people to fly to the moon." The cynic in me is never one hundred percent sure whether this actually happened or not – although even if it didn't, I like to think that every janitor at NASA since this story first appeared on the internet has requested that this phrase be included in their own job description! Even if it's just folklore, it's a wonderful story which illustrates the point that you don't need to be the person flying the shuttle or firing up the engine to feel 'part of something'.

Most of us aren't in the business of sending people to the moon. But then most people aren't running a business and making all the decisions either. In a business which provides, for example, creative services to the financial sector, for an employee who works in a non-client-facing role, you have to look differently at summarising how someone's role impacts the organisation.

On a practical basis, you can include this in every job description or advert you place. We always encourage people to start any job description they write by having the first line say just that: *The purpose of your role is to xxxxx.* It is a simple but effective way of highlighting that although someone's day-to-day tasks will vary (and may sometimes be a bit monotonous), they are all needed and they contribute to something much bigger.

Encouraging collaboration and teamwork among your team members also helps create this meaning in a regular way. Only when every person works together can the magic happen: from the person who greets the customer in their first touchpoint to the people who put together their products, packs up their socks, cartridges or flowers to the one who follows up to make sure they have what they need and they are happy.

You can also reinforce the significance of their work by communicating clearly with your team in one-on-one meetings and by addressing questions such as:

- How much freedom and independence do they have in their role?
- What kind of support do they provide that is valued by customers or other teams?
- What strengths do they have that can be utilised more to benefit the business?

By discussing these points on a regular basis, people not only see the value of their contributions and how their work positively impacts the team and the business as a whole, they also see you appreciating it too, which can be extremely motivating.

What have you done today *(to make you feel proud)*?

Strengths-based feedback – where you focus on the strengths of an individual rather than spending too much time trying to increase their skills in the parts of their job that they're a bit weaker on – can also help reinforce the meaning of work to your team.

Whether from your own observation, general feedback from others or your team themselves, being open about which bits of their work they enjoy more and are better at can help supersize these strengths and encourage even more of them.

Regular one-to-one conversations and questions to uncover the satisfaction people feel can also be great opportunities to remind the team of the impact they have and why they matter. Or as Heather Small would sing, *"What have you done today to make you feel proud?"*

These are the things people will smile about when they think of their work. It can make them feel more fulfilled. It makes them feel that even if it's not their mission in life to create carpet fibres or sell events or ensure that software works without bugs (or whatever the forte of your business happens to be), they are doing 'something' which resonates. It may be that helping people, serving others or working in an industry strikes the right chord. *Or it may just be that they like working for you and your team...*

Without these reminders and reinforcements of what matters to you and the business, people can be left feeling uninspired at best or - *at worst* - demotivated.

The £100 million mirage

There are business owners I've worked with and for in the past who feel that meaning can come solely from their financial target: they use their company valuation or their sales figures to try to motivate and inspire their team.

Whilst I'm all for goals (in fact, I'm about to go deep on them in the next chapter), I have a problem with that train of thought.

Just having a number as your target is not a good thing in my book. As was the case for those who were disappointed in Deep Thought's answer to the meaning of life, it's difficult to find meaning in a number. They don't matter when there's no context.

Setting your growth number to hit £5 million or £10 million revenue means little to most of your employees unless *a)* they have such a significant number of share options that they will work all day, every day to receive them, or *b)* they are not telling you the truth.

In one business I worked with, the CEO's goal was to have a £100 million valuation. Nothing wrong with that as it lined up with some of his own goals and what he wanted in his life. The challenge was that for everyone else, it didn't mean a thing. Everyone in the business knew that when this person insisted on everyone focusing only on revenue numbers, hitting this number resulted in a bonus... just for him!

Demotivating? *Check.* Meaningless? *Check.*

Focus instead on what makes your business special *behind* the number and you'll find that people will flock to it.

Your Action:

1. Jot down a few words to describe what you want your business to be known for and its main purpose (beyond making money).
2. Bake in what you find important within different communication mediums to ensure people know them. One of our clients starts every internal meeting with their goals to remind people 'why' they're there.
3. Make it relevant to your team by including in their job description details of their contribution and purpose and (when it comes to it) their own goals and focus.
4. Reinforce the meaning in their work by asking your team what they've done recently that they feel proud of.
5. Recognise your team when they align by reminding them who they are helping and why this matters (the impact).

---

[1] *Help Your Employees Find Purpose or Watch Them Leave,* McKinsey, Naina Dhingra, Andrew Samo, Bill Schaninger, and Matt Schrimper
[2] *Putting Purpose to Work*, PWC, June 2016
[3] ONS - *Vacancies and Jobs in the UK:* June 2023

4
Accountability

I've been working with businesses for over twenty-five years now: small ones, large ones, fast-growing ones, declining ones... And whilst having meaning in your work is a critical ingredient in creating magic with your team, all the meaning in the world can't make the action happen on its own.

Company Y appeared full of meaning when I met them: they had a clear purpose, they had cash flow in the bank to back up their plans and they had some team members in place ready to rock and roll. On paper, it should have been happy days. However, the CEO confided in me that something was amiss.

Talking to people didn't initially yield any obvious answers as everyone seemed quite keen, happy, knowledgeable and engaged. But slowly I started to notice some oddities. In any senior team meetings, the boss would start by giving an update on things and then swiftly move on to chatting about life, love and the universe. No-one was pressed for any details other than *How's it going?* Everyone had a very nice conversation about what they were up to and then they moved on.

Often these meetings were deferred anyway due to some operational emergency or other. No-one really cared about the meeting or pushed for it as they never had much to say anyhow, and it became clear that there was no forum for seeing who was responsible for what. This metaphorical ship was rudderless. Any direction the business had started out with was being lost amongst a mix of day-to-day issues and pleasantries, without tackling anything that was going to help the business grow and move forward. In essence, the summary of most of these updates sounded like, "The dog ate my homework." Or rather, "Someone else's dog ate my homework."

These were intelligent people tasked with things which were easily within their capabilities, yet progress was not being made at the rate it needed to be and unless they upped the ante considerably, the end of their runway would be soon upon them.

Speaking further to those in the room after that first meeting, they showed no malice but were confused over who was doing what and when things had to be done by and expressed a startling denial that they shouldered any responsibility for what was falling apart around them. They said they didn't feel that they had agency to make changes or decisions and therefore all that seemed to be left was a growing indifference.

Where once they had cared about what was going on around them, as they became more disengaged they were happy for all decisions and progress to fall on the CEO and a few others: becoming ghost employees, so to speak.

This showed me that even if your teams have all the meaning in the world, your business still needs some other important ingredients for performance to peak. Number one in this instance was getting some accountability in place.

Owning it

The world has gone slightly mad for accountability in recent years and the word dominates social media and the business press. I knew what the word meant a while ago; however, the boom in the coaching industry particularly has expanded this further and accountability is now often seen as a by-word for success with 'accountability groups' springing up right, left and centre.

Once the domain of business, there are now all sorts of personal accountability groups you can join with ease: for the exercise you do, the food you eat, and the drink you drink (and don't drink). Hell, you can even have them for your parenting skills or your marriage.

We are not quite at 'unprecedented' levels of use of the word yet, but it's not far off.

What does the word actually mean however? Why is it so important to have accountability as a core principle within a business? And why, when the term is used so much, do so many businesses suck at achieving any form of it?

The dictionary definition of *accountability* is: 'the fact of being responsible for what you do and able to give a satisfactory reason for it, or the degree to which this happens'.

My lay(wo)man definition, however, is that having accountability means you 'own it' *(where 'it' is whatever you've committed to doing).*

In a business, this means everyone is clear about who is responsible for what. They also understand and accept the fact that if they fail to deliver on those responsibilities – *in some form or other* – they will be evaluated on that. It means that when things go south, no-one rushes to blame another team or throws their hands in the air in a *'not my problem, mate'* kind of way or pushes off responsibilities onto the person sitting next to them, but acknowledges that it was their responsibility and is transparent about what happened.

In business owner terms, by the way, accountability can also be described as the answer to the question, *"How do I get my team to do as I bloody well ask?"*

People are given responsibilities because they're trusted to deliver on them. As Spiderman would say, *"With great power comes great responsibility."* So whilst the output of an evaluation may vary tremendously from company to company, it's important that team members understand that consequences will come from not meeting those responsibilities and that they're not given them for the sheer hell of it.

At an individual level, people enjoy having responsibilities. Knowing what is expected of them versus the next person in your business gives them autonomy and encourages them to deliver what they've said they'll do. From an organisational standpoint, you need to know that each part of the business is delivering what you need and is functioning as it should: from who owns your sales strategy to who delivers your marketing implementation and your customer service.

Without a strong sense of people 'owning it' in your business, at best you can see duplication of effort and time wasted in coordination efforts across teams. At worst, passing off and apathy can run riot, leaving an incredibly disengaged team.

Keep calm and stay accountable

When you 'own' the things you are tasked with, do practical things to reinforce this, including sharing what you're focused on, giving updates on what is happening, and communicating how things are progressing so everyone is aware of any potential blockers. Essentially, do what you say you will and you will build up a bank of trust with others. Trust is unwritten in any employment contract or job description, yet is a basic requirement of any successful employment relationship.

The river of trust needs to flow *all* ways: the team needs to trust you; you need to trust the team; they need to trust each other. When people don't feel they can rely on others, overall performance will suffer.

Greater accountability helps generate this trust. But more than that, it also leads to greater results and a greater sense of happiness. A strong sense of accountability in your business creates a sense of calm for you that can only come about when you know all areas are covered.

As a business owner, you take a natural (and sometimes, let's face it, unhealthy!) interest in what's going on in all parts of your business and it can stress you out when you can't see what's taking place or when things aren't being done. *It can feel like you're losing a bit of 'control'.*

Accountability, however, shines the light on what is going on in the business without the need for constant checking and therefore increases your trust in the team.

In principle, of course, it sounds so easy: once responsibilities are divided up, we just explain what we're focused on and then everyone does it. Bingo!

However, even when you practise accountability in a consistent way, this can become more challenging as your business grows. Just think about your locations for one thing: one minute you're all together in the shared office workspace listening in on each others' calls, calling out on a daily basis what needs to be done and understanding *almost by osmosis* what is happening in every part of the business; the next minute every task seems to take twice as long.

Don't forget to 'ask for the task'

In order to make accountability a reality for your business, the number one thing you need to do is be clear on what you expect from your team. You can't be expected to know telepathically what your customers want, so why should you expect your team to be any different? Avoidance of making your expectations clear not only makes it difficult for people to live up to your expectations, it also makes it difficult for you to have any real comeback on anyone when they explain (quite rightly) that they didn't know what they were supposed to be doing in the first place.

When looking at your customers, one of the golden rules is not to forget to 'ask for the sale', of course. *What do you want the customer to buy/do next?* With your team it is much the same: they like to know what's expected of them so don't forget to 'ask for the task' and let them know what you want them to do with absolute clarity.

I know that you typically hire educated people into your team and you might ask a question of us – *surely at that level, they should know what they're meant to be doing?*

Even with great qualifications, a strong sense of initiative and a lot of experience in different organisations, people can find themselves with their eyes and action trained in the wrong direction if you don't set expectations of what success looks like for you in this regard. Many times, I have seen a nearly 'superstar' performer reduced to *'a bit of a disappointment'* in the words of their boss because the team member failed to live up to the standards the business owner felt were promised in the recruitment stages. But you must ask yourself at this stage whether you gave them the right direction in the first place.

You can obviously use documents such as your job descriptions or roles and responsibilities to support this clarity, but nothing creates clarity and builds the trust you need for them to own it in the way you need them to, as verbally communicating this.

Knowing your OKRs from your elbow

Clarity on this, as with all good things in business, typically starts with you. It starts with you being clear to the team about what they can expect from you: be clear about what you are trying to achieve, what you will do for them and how you will behave.

We tend to see this first as outcomes - *the results you want to see in terms of customer numbers, processing times, output of code, systems launched, people hired, etc.* It is what you want and when you want it done by. Given that we know business owners tend to be an excitable bunch with lots of plans and ideas, sometimes this can be a very long list indeed.

When it comes to the outcomes, the targets or the goals you want to focus on, try to narrow it down to your top three (or - go on - five if you must!). They show others what you care about most. Then keep on reinforcing the hell out of these areas to stress the importance of them to your team.

One client of mine has what they term a ‘hit list’: just three things they keep up on their whiteboard for anyone who comes in their office to see, the top three things they are working on at any given point. It is relaxed and clear, but it sends the message of where you are focused.

In the early years of my career, I was accustomed to creating and working toward objectives: I knew they should be SMART (Specific, Measurable, Achievable, Realistic and Timebound); I saw the value in having these on a personal basis and I trained people in a number of businesses on how to create and achieve them. Such was the drilling about having SMART objectives, that many people could recite them at the drop of a hat and even if they were incredibly bored with the terms themselves, they knew the drill about what was expected of them.

Some tried their hand at KPIs (Key Performance Indicators) – another form of management measurement that many organisations commonly worked towards – whilst others stuck to the solid ‘Goals’ or Targets.

And just when we felt we were getting along fine and putting them in the boring-but-important category, along came Google with their fancy OKRs (Objectives and Key Results). Hey presto, objectives became sexy again! *Or at least as sexy as objectives can be...*

OKRs are not a 'new thing' and Google didn't invent OKRs themselves. They were an adaptation of the objective setting method John Doerr used whilst at Intel. In waxing lyrical about how they were being used to power one of the fastest-growing businesses in the world, interest in them spiked. In the process of doing so, however, they also caused a bit of confusion. *What's the difference between a Goal and an OKR?* Well, none in my mind, I'm afraid. If you've written a solid goal which has measurable success criteria (which includes time and other SMART parameters), then you have yourself an OKR right there. Sure, some purists say that OKRs should only be designed to be 80 percent achievable versus Goals being either met or not met, but in my experience, this sort of detail only adds to the confusion and puts another blocker in the way of people progressing and building accountability.

OKRs are just Goals by another name, so if nothing else, I implore you to not get muddled by the lingo and titles you attach to whichever form of goal setting you want to follow. *Your employees don't care a hoot about these anyhow.* Make sure you get one of them in place. Whilst your teams do not care about which method you use, what they *do* care about is consistency, so once you've settled on one title, try not to switch.

My view is that if I'm setting expectations for team members about what I want to see happen, I personally prefer the term *objectives* as I find the term requires less explanation than others and is the most common denominator for people.

A slight note of caution before we leave this section: there will be many of you reading this who have Perfect Peter or Polly tendencies. Fortunately, I am not cursed with this trait. However, I have worked with many who are and I have seen the impact on their teams when someone feels that they should be one hundred percent perfect in order to progress on it.

I'm sorry to say, for accountability and performance purposes at least, it never will be.

I have seen and been involved with countless performance processes. Despite hours and hours of effort, training and communication, the perfect art of cascading goals may still elude you. This is because, despite all our best efforts, this is not an exact science... people are still involved.

The good news is that although the perfect waterfall cannot usually be found outside of a slide deck, this doesn't diminish the success of those who set out their intentions, work through the process and achieve the magic without gold-plating it!

It ain't what you do it's the way that you do it

It's not only the outcomes and results in financial or customer terms *(i.e. the hard metrics)* that you should look at when it comes to accountability. In any business, it is just as important to be clear on the kind of behaviour you expect from your team in achieving these. It is not just the 'what' but the 'how' you do things.

I know of companies that have become unstuck when the behaviour of members of the team has been at odds with what is expected in their business, rather than because of a problem with the results they've seen, so don't underestimate the importance of these in your success (*or failure)* as a team.

Values and behaviours can be articulated at a company level to surface how you expect people to behave and what standards you expect them to uphold. Also, whether you like it or not, you are their role model in your business. How you behave shows others what your values are, regardless of what you have written on the wall.

In the same way those of you who are parents may have been startled when you first recognised in your child a pattern of behaviour that you exhibit yourself, after you have acted in a certain way for a while in your business, other members of your team will start to copy it. This is great if you're a proud 'parent' and are happy to see this behaviour emulated across the business to positive effect. But what if there's the occasional personality trait you'd rather wasn't replicated across the business?

Do you not always bother to follow up on things you've promised? Your team will start to do the same. *Do you not accept responsibility when something goes wrong and look to blame others?* Ditto. In parent/child terms, you'd be chuffed to bits if you saw your child help another child up but less so if you saw them help themselves to their toys whilst they were playing with them.

In one company I've worked with, the CEO was highly results-focused and keen on driving an agenda of accountability, but undermined this with his habit of picking on members of his management team in their monthly meetings and publicly scrutinising their updates to make his point: questions were always asked in a tone which made the recipient feel about two inches tall; new questions were fired off without time to answer the first one; his behaviour drove grown professional adults to tears of humiliation. These meetings filled people with dread as they would do anything to avoid having the laser focused on them and the upshot was that far from bringing issues to his attention to try to solve problems that arose in the business, people tried to bury bad news or actively blame others for lack of progress. Results spiralled. He refused to see that not only was he making this kind of behaviour acceptable and even encouraged in the business, but that it was stopping the very accountability he was seeking.

Conversely, another leader I've worked with was a master of driving accountability across the business, even without a clear set of formal objectives for everyone. To achieve this he made sure that he spent time with everyone in the business, making sure they understood what they were responsible for, talking to them about what they needed to focus on, allowing them to be clear on what autonomy they had and thanking them for their contribution. When something went wrong, he would always start a discussion with a version of *'this one's on me'* by reassuring the team that it was his overall responsibility but that he wanted to understand and learn from everything that had happened in order to avoid it happening again and focus on what needed to be done to move the dial. In fact, not many things did go wrong in that business, as people felt such a sense of pride in what they were doing that they worked night and day to come up with ideas and deliver over and above what was needed.

On a day-to-day basis therefore, very simple things such as asking how others are doing, speaking in a respectful way, being patient with people and so on are all things people want to see in their leaders and which will be emulated across your team. The other kinds of behaviour, micromanaging, being closed off and (God forbid) shouting, can be irritating at best and destructive at worst.

Both leaders had the same focus on results yet two very different outcomes for their organisations: it ain't what you do, but the way that you do it.

Best of intentions

You've laid out what you want the team to focus on, and you've been clear on what you expect. Now is surely the time to sit back and watch the magic happen. *Not quite...*

It seems so simple, yet the world over, people struggle to do what they say they're going to do: be it training to run a 10K or aligning their team and ensuring that everyone is pulling their weight. As I mentioned earlier, there are whole industries dedicated to holding people accountable and making sure they do what they're supposed to do and many people pay vast amounts to others to keep them in check.

We're all very good at setting out with the best of intentions – especially so when we're asked to commit by our boss – but less good at delivering on them. In your own business, just because Alex in Marketing *says* they are going to deliver hundreds of new leads to your sales team within the next month and up the ante by getting a thousand more subscribers to your social channels, this doesn't automatically mean it's going to happen.

The challenge is to keep people focused, keep the momentum up on these intentions, keep track of all the progress people make, and allow a chance for others to do so too. Luckily, this doesn't need to be excessively complicated.

I can see you!

There's no point in having all these really great goals and intentions if you hide them away. We are forgetful folks, and we need to keep things at the forefront of our minds in order for them to really 'bed in'. For this, we need transparency.

Allowing transparency on what people are doing and how they are getting on is a key way to help accountability: if you encourage people to share their progress by doing so yourself first then it becomes your modus operandi.

On a day-to-day basis at The HR Hub, we use one open email to communicate with our clients. I borrowed and adapted the idea early on from one of my own clients and quite honestly, I can't imagine how we could manage without this. In the team, it not only enables us to naturally pick up what's going on with each of our clients so everyone understands the broader landscape (which saves us oodles of time) but also means there is less likelihood of us missing something as there are multiple sets of eyes on things. When people first start doing this, it can feel weird. After all, we're used to using email in a one-on-one situation and it might make you feel like you are being spied on or your work is being checked. However, once you've got over that and recognise that it's a good thing, it becomes an internal sense check on the quality of work. After all, if you've got multiple sets of eyes on things, you certainly want to come across well! It becomes completely unnoticeable. It becomes 'just the way we do things'.

It works the same way if you are encouraging accountability from an objective setting perspective. Outside of the day-to-day, there are a lot of ways to support and achieve this, from the very basic but effective shared online documents such as Google Sheets and Office365 right through to dedicated software such as Lattice, Leapsome or 7Geese. There is no right way of doing this, although a word of caution in terms of jumping in with any software and thinking it will solve your accountability issues. I have found that even if it has all the functionality in the world, if you haven't got the behaviour and support matched in your business that you want to show, it might be a waste of money and time.

Consider the case of two different businesses I spent time with, both in the tech space, both very conversant with any technology and considered themselves to be relatively early adopters.

Take Business One: the CEO wanted to launch a performance management system as they believed that having this rigour in objective setting was a core business practice. They were also keen as mustard to have software to support this and wanted to ensure that all the systems worked together. They invested in a brand-new system which included an HR module and linked multiple systems across consulting, finance, etc. This business wasn't extremely large at the time (nearing sixty-five people) but it was drilled into everyone that they were all expected to complete their objectives in the system and share with tracking to take place every quarter. If nothing was shared, it would be highlighted to the CEO due to a lack of visibility. Everyone could see the FD's objectives just as clearly as the Sales support engineer and because it was part of how they 'managed things', it helped everyone align behind what they were trying to achieve. There was no guesswork and no-one felt particularly like this was a big brother. However, it became a routine that helped the business become extremely successful. In fact, I'd wager they're still using a version of the system now.

Compare this with Business Two which also wanted to launch a performance management process but who were more interested in the tech side of things. Everyone loved the system and it was super-easy to implement, yet many on the leadership team weren't too keen on writing objectives themselves, or indeed following up with any progress on them when they did. Several months into this launch, following training and communications, they finally admitted defeat and realised this software was never going to change their behaviour - regardless of how amazing it was!

Get the behaviours aligned to how you want them in your business and *then* usher in the tech.

The secret to great accountability is... timing

When encouraging people to be accountable, cadence is often another thing that comes up: *how often should we check in to see what's going on?* Too often and it feels like micromanagement; too far apart and it seems like you don't care.

Well, the ideal answer is in real-time: when you make things as transparent as possible, you don't always need to meet to see how things are progressing (take my example of shared emails above). However, given that the human touch helps people feel supported in what they're trying to achieve and it's a big ask to expect people to update their progress each day, I consider that check-ins and updates should be at least weekly between you and your direct reports for day-to-day things with this perhaps extended to a monthly update for those longer-term goals people are working to. Ultimately, the more regularly you check in on people, the better. Research has shown that when people see the progress they are making in anything - *at work or in their personal lives* - they become more motivated to continue. It reinforces their intent in a way that a set of objectives languishing in a drawer somewhere or in the lesser-used drive on their laptop never can!

Obviously, the easier you make this, the more likely people are to get into the groove. To achieve this, some companies I work with adopt a traffic light system for displaying the progress against their objectives, which has proved effective – or they verbally share on a 'stand up' call with their team. You can use simple language to let people know where progress is being made and where there are blockers: Red = Help! Orange = getting there; Green = we're flying, thanks!

Whatever groove you choose, it needs to be right for your business and manageable for you.

Whilst all the evidence and anecdotes point to accountability thriving if you put these kinds of systems in place, the other reason you do it is to catch things when they don't go to plan. Not so that you can harangue people when they do go off-course but so that any issues and errors surface so that you can learn and do better.

Accountability doesn't mean hauling anyone over the coals when someone hasn't achieved what they set out to do, but it does mean that when this does happen, it's going to be visible. And when that is clear, how you handle it will say a lot about your style.

Uh oh – something's gone wrong

Occasionally, despite all the things you put in place, you may see that the performance isn't moving as fast as you hoped or indeed at all. This is possibly the number one concern that our clients raise with us in one form or another.

The first question I ask when it has been explained that someone hasn't been pulling their weight is, "Do they know what they are supposed to be doing?" (see above) The second question is, "Have you spoken to them about it?" *Yes* and *No* are the typical answers I receive, or sometimes, when we drill it down, "*Yes, I've spoken to them, but not really.*"

It is almost understandable. We shy away from anything that looks like conflict for the most part. However, holding people to account shouldn't mean you need to don your flak jacket to hold a conversation about it, let alone put on your helmet. There are people I know who are quite happy to tear a strip off their waiting staff should they be served the wrong drink in a restaurant, yet will do anything in their power to avoid speaking directly to their team if they spot that their written communication is not strong enough or they are taking too long to do a task. Whilst neither of these is ideal behaviour, it seems odd that they can come hand in hand. They're quite happy to give negative feedback when they may not see someone again but struggle to fit it into a working relationship.

If this is you, I urge you as a starting point to get comfortable with addressing issues early and don't let them fester. After all, it's much easier to say to someone when you spot it, *"Hey, I noticed earlier this afternoon when you responded to Client X, that you used last year's pricing list. Can you send them an update or make sure you use the most up-to-date one next time?"* It doesn't cause offence and it's likely the person will say, *"Whoops – so sorry, you're right,"* and then get back to the client as soon as possible and check twice the next time. Plus, if you do this in a forum where you chat a lot, others can avoid making the same error as well.

Peer feedback is when people sense check each other's work. It is another way to encourage greater accountability and many software developers include it as a formal step in their workflow. I also actively encourage it in my business as there is quite a lot of nuance in our work and it's good for another reader to check that we have the right 'tone' as well as fact.

When there are more serious performance concerns or when someone is persistently not doing as they say they will, you may need to address it in a different way. However, I would advise caution in jumping to a formal process straight away.

Performance improvement processes have their time and place – they can be very useful tools to structure discussions – but I could count the successful 'performance improvement processes' in all my time on one hand, so they should be used with care. This is mostly due to the fact that if you jump to using a 'process' straight away, perhaps as a means to avoid giving feedback in general, it has the overlaying effect of seeming hollow and making someone feel they are being 'watched' the whole time without any of the upsides. As we know from our own motivation when we feel like we are being micromanaged, it's the number one turnoff for people and may just send someone the other way entirely.

My initial suggestion is to address the person informally by being clear on the issues you see, stating their impact and then asking the team member to make the changes.

Feedback has a clear role here and whilst some people feel more comfortable giving feedback than others, this is often just down to practice. I would urge you to get into the habit of giving feedback as much as possible, as it is a game changer in terms of being able to have open discussions with people. One way to encourage others to do this is to seek feedback yourself – *quite possibly publicly* – by asking others what more they think you can do, or how well they think you have done on *x*. It is often quite scary for business owners to do this, but if you can be open to receiving this and can listen without either being defensive or listening to respond, it's a great way to encourage others to do the same.

Some businesses I've worked with love the idea of 'radical candour', a type of feedback made famous by Kim Scott's book of the same title. This form of feedback is more brutally honest than most and the idea behind it is that everyone knows it is done to be supportive. In normalising this kind of frankness, it gets to the heart of issues very quickly and allows people to grow quicker. The challenge with this kind of behaviour, however, is that to be very radical in your candour requires a tonne of trust and skill to be present in both giving and receiving this feedback. Given that people find it hard enough to give feedback to a waiter about their food *("Everything is fine,"* they say as they're mentally writing their two-star Trip Advisor review) let alone give feedback to their team, I confess that I've never seen this adopted successfully company-wide and nor is it something I would completely encourage either. In small groups of people who've known each other for a long time and where the trust has been built, definitely. But for those who are just forming their team, where their communication skills still need some work or where teams are more disjointed, I'd give it a wide berth.

This doesn't mean, of course, that you should avoid giving any feedback.

How you keep people accountable has ramifications: if you ignore poor performance, then you are encouraging everyone to let quality and issues slide. After all, if you don't care if deadlines are met or the service you're providing is weak, then why would anyone else? In this sense, you risk weakening your own reputation and that of your business.

Accountability brings so many benefits that it's worth the effort to make it part of your Modus Operandi. Say goodbye to tricky performances and conversations and hello to the magical feeling of knowing everyone's got it covered!

Your Action:

1. Be clear on what you expect from your team *in both results and behaviour.* Set clear expectations of these through role modelling as well as in writing.
2. Don't get caught up in the lingo of what you're going to measure; put that effort into making it part of 'the way you do things'.
3. Be as transparent as possible in your systems and processes: from objective setting to everyday actions.
4. Don't forget to follow up with people once their intentions are set: you need regular cadence to check that people are doing what they said they would.
5. Own your own mistakes (as publicly as possible): playing the blame game, whether by passing the buck externally or passively stitching up a co-worker by not standing up for them, is a no-no!

5
Growth

In the previous chapter, I highlighted the importance of setting intentions for your team and then encouraging ownership. It would be unusual for growth not to feature as part of this process and these conversations. Whether you want to acquire clients, move into markets or just make a straightforward increase in ££s, progress is a desirable quality for you, your team and (if you have any) your investors.

Hardwired into all of us is an inherent desire to grow and develop. This drive is a powerful internal motivator that probably prompted you to subscribe to the podcast which you fell asleep to last night, to invest in a business coach or personal trainer or maybe even to pick up this book to learn something you didn't know before. Whatever the specifics are for you, the action you take comes from your desire to keep evolving.

Most businesses see two kinds of growth: that of the business itself and that of the people within it. In an ideal world, they happen side by side and symbiotically: harness the former and you see results in the latter. And whilst not every business needs (or wants) a career framework for every role or a competency-based formula for job promotions, one of the quickest ways to make your business grow is to **support your team in developing their knowledge, skills and experience.**

For a business where there is Meaning attached to it *(rather than just growth for growth's sake)* it seems obvious why growth is beneficial: more growth = greater impact, investment opportunities and success. More fuel for the future, so to speak.

And whilst your business's growth can often be measured in objective terms - process efficiencies, number of clients, revenues, etc. - for *people*, whilst growth is just as important and meaningful, individual and professional growth is intrinsic and therefore a little harder to define... It's an ethereal phenomenon, very occasionally measured by numbers *(e.g. books read, qualifications earned, job title changed)* but more often by just a feeling we have with regards to our progression, promotion or simply learning something we didn't know the day before.

This seeking of growth is part of the reason some estimates put the global personal development market at USD 41.81 billion in 2021 *(yes, billion!)* [1] and why Statista finds that the personal training industry in the UK alone has seen a rise from 2012 to 2020 of 30 percent. [2]

Be it our brains or our biceps, we all seemingly want to become that little bit bigger, better and brighter.

It's also the reason why **Growth is the third principle to embrace when creating the MAGIC in your teams.**

Exit Stage Left

Last year, one of our clients asked us to undertake some interviews with departing team members and uncover some insight: they'd had some higher than typical employee turnover and – particularly given that they had a good reputation in the market, treated their teams well and seemed to have a clear purpose – the reason for the exodus was puzzling and they wanted to understand what might be fuelling this.

After several conversations, on examining the data we found that although a lot of key areas had been covered in terms of their strategy to 'find and keep' great people, it appeared that the 'grow' stage of any lifecycle had been slightly overlooked. The lack of development opportunities was the number one common denominator for people handing in their notice. *"I'm bored,"* or, *"I just want to try something new,"* were phrases we heard repeated in one form or another. Whilst it was true that people were treated well by the company and liked their jobs, they didn't seem to feel there was any obvious answer to the question, *"Where am I going next?"*

Even if your issues are not quite the same as this business's or if you're not losing team members at a rate which keeps you up at night, holding on to the team you have is often one of the top three 'People' goals any business has: after all, the chances are you've spent a lot of time and effort getting them there in the first place. And whilst it can sometimes feel like a guessing game in terms of what's going to help people in your business stay *(case in point that none of the team members we spoke to had raised any concerns with their managers or the business owner about their lack of progress in this particular situation)*, our experience from being involved in hundreds more such exit interviews, engagement surveys and conversations with employees such as those in this company, is that there is no question that working in a place where growth and progression are valued and encouraged, helps people want to stay with you.

Professor Teresa Amabile and Steven Kramer offer one explanation for this in their book: *The Progress Principle: Using Small Wins to Ignite Joy, Engagement, and Creativity at Work, 2011* [3]. In this research (and subsequent articles), they share their fundamental theory that we are all motivated by progress of some kind which we need to recognise as happening. Stay stuck and our motivation plummets. But keep moving - *even if it's not in one single direction or in significant steps* - and just the feeling of learning can send our motivation soaring.

We advised this particular client who was suffering from too many team members jumping ship, that instead of throwing lots of time and effort into guessing which areas of development they needed to focus on to stem the exiting flow, to simply switch the interviews back a gear and start holding 'stay interviews'.

A 'stay interview' is very similar to an 'exit interview' and is typically held by an individual's manager with the objective of understanding what keeps the person working for them so they can do more of it. Knowing that growth and development were key reasons for our clients' employees leaving, we suggested they focus on those areas to ensure they stayed engaged. The questions we proposed asking were almost identical to those asked in an 'exit interview', just with a different slant: rather than asking, "How ***did*** you feel about your opportunities for growth and development?" we asked, "How ***do*** you feel about your opportunities for growth and development?"

You can, of course, ask these kinds of questions in survey format online, which is very time-efficient. But doing it this way misses the opportunity to strengthen your relationships and show your interest in what this person's idea of progress looks like. Growth has such a personal meaning to each individual – one person's career motorway is another person's cul-de-sac – that it's worth taking the time to understand what this means to them and crucially, how it can be aligned with the role that they are in now and what they can take on in the future.

The outcome was that these conversations – *held particularly with those who were considered the key players they most wanted to hold on to* – allowed them to probe into the areas of learning people were most interested in and drove the subsequent development plans they put in place to great effect.

Tomorrow's World

Keeping hold of your team isn't the only reason to spend time looking at their growth. For purely selfish reasons if for no other, you actually need their growth to keep your business on track too.

When I started up The HR Hub many years ago, I was already pretty skilled in the area of HR and People, just as you are in your field. Whilst I envisaged the business expanding, I still hadn't quite clocked what this would mean for my own growth and development. I was confident in interviewing, implementing a new performance management system, advising over thorny employee relations or creating a people plan which would scale. This was all well and good. But before I knew it, as I acquired more clients, then more staff, there were all these other areas I was distinctly less confident and skilled in that I hadn't quite envisaged I would need.

Accounting, marketing, analysis, website design, sales and systems *(for just about everything you can think of)* are just some of the areas I'd never touched before but which I've had a crack at in the last few years. In all these areas, including those I could have happily avoided, not only did I find that I needed more of these skills than I had thought I would in order to keep growing, it turned out that I needed to keep building on them continuously just to avoid falling behind. And even then, new ones were always popping up!

Even when you have the very best of intentions and focus, unexpected challenges and demands continue to raise their heads, whack-a-mole style, leaving you scrambling to address them with limited resources and time. No matter how prepared you are, the reality often is that there isn't enough of 'you' to fill all the gaps that keep opening up.

Even your best-laid plans which mean you have in hand all the skills you need in your business today may need to shift gears and adapt to something you didn't see coming.

On 30 November 2022, a new chatbot app was launched. It would quickly become part of our work, our lives and, let's face it, our vocabulary.

For many of us at the time, even with the abundance of articles published on the topic of Artificial Intelligence (AI) and a range of AI tools already on the market, using AI in our day-to-day business still seemed like the stuff of Tomorrow's World. If I had said that this chatbot would gain one hundred million users in its first six months, become the fastest-growing app of all time and be used by everyone, many would still have said sceptically, "*ChatGPWhat?*"

Be it in employment or in schools *(good luck with being an examiner right now!)*, "I ChatGPTed it," has become a common phrase. For many roles - *marketing, customer service, content creation, the list goes on* - being able to adopt the use of this and other AI tools rapidly will give any business a clear competitive advantage over those that don't. Whilst applying AI skills might not have been needed in your toolkit this time last year, as I write this, these skills are already being seen in adverts and job descriptions.

It isn't only new technology in which your teams need to keep skilled up: trends driven by external events can change your industry. Or perhaps you and your team are innovating better ways to deliver your product or services and 'being the change' yourselves. Either way, **your business growth depends on your team growing the skills to meet these needs.** Even the most flush of businesses can't just hire a new person every time they need to do something differently.

Not just for billionaires

Keeping your teams firing on all cylinders and growing your business skills to *adapt* to the future are reasons enough to have **growth as a key ingredient for employee magic**. But even if they weren't, another reason is making sure you have the right people and skills in place to *run it* in the future.

One of our clients – a highly successful tech consulting firm – prioritised building a succession plan for their CEO whilst only in their second year of business. They employed thirty-five people at the time, and many would have thought it low on the long list of HR and People planning activities taking place. However, fast forward five years, the CEO is suitably independent from the day-to-day running of the business – so much so that without him there would be two other very capable people ready and able to steer the ship. With investors vying for their business, it's easy to see just how well their strategy paid off from a value perspective.

For those new to HR and People-speak, succession planning is the process of identifying talent needed and developing skills for future leadership positions. It is working out who you think could do key roles in your business with you, for you or – *if you're planning to exit pretty soon* – when you're out of the picture. You have a plan in place to make sure they're able to step up when they're needed.

A recent award-winning and popular TV show, *Succession*, highlights this specific business practice and shines a light on what one such *highly unusual* process can look like. The show opens with the fictional patriarch of a wealthy media family, Roy Logan, declaring he is going to step down from his global empire and that he'll nominate his successor shortly. What follows is a family drama full of twists and turns that would shame even Shakespeare's imagination, as his children and partners connive to undercut and oust each other as contenders in the quest to be the 'chosen one'. Whilst there isn't a whole stack of best practice 'leadership skills' you'd be advised to adopt from these episodes or that anyone with a CIPD qualification would recommend *(although you'll learn a lot about what not to do!)*, the one thing you can take from it is that planning your exit isn't always that simple. It is best to have in mind plans B, C and D.

Succession planning in its simplest form rests on three basic principles: first identify the key roles you want a backup for; then identify people in your business who display the skills and potential to fill these roles in the future; finally shift the focus to helping those people grow by providing solid learning and development opportunities that equip them to do their own jobs as well as learn for the future.

Identifying the key roles is typically the quickest part of this process. Look for those which impact the success of the business most or notice which people have specific technical skills you would find difficult to replace. Identifying the people who display the skills and potential can take slightly longer. It involves looking at your whole team to assess not just their current skills, but who has the potential to be successful in a different role. You may have a 'gut feel' for some of those who have potential, but I encourage you to look at whatever data you have on your team's performance – appraisals, customer and 360 feedback etc. – to inject more objectivity into the process and highlight anyone who may be less obvious.

One client of mine has had particular success with identifying people who can take on leadership roles by considering someone's general performance and impact, irrespective of the role they have been undertaking in the business. This has allowed them to fill several key roles from unexpected corners of the business as they grow whilst keeping the mix of external hires to a minimum: from consulting into people leadership and development into sales. By opening their mind to consider all high performers, as opposed to only those in the functions of the roles they're looking for successors in, they have spotted potential that might otherwise have been missed.

Once you have identified them, you can help these successors and heirs apparent grow. You can do this in a number of ways. Occasionally you may want a formal programme of learning. However, smaller firms often do this by sharing the core skills (e.g. commercial awareness, financial understanding, etc.) that are required to drive the business and then supporting the learning of those skills through a mix of methods including mentoring, coaching and the opportunity to test out their new-found skills in different situations on-the-job.

If you're just starting out or if everything is going swimmingly and you're not looking for a shift in structure, planning for successors may seem inconceivable right now. However, those five to ten years that you marked against your business plans can whizz by before you know it. If you hope your future involves a buy-out, sale, or just stepping back a bit, you should consider removing yourself from the day-to-day decision making and being the single-point-of-blockage as a priority. Not only will it allow you to test how it functions without you and close those gaps, a business which doesn't need you to run it will ultimately increase in health and wealth.

Succession planning, after all, isn't just for billionaires.

Finding the sweet spot

If the idea of mapping out a growth plan for every member of your team however fills you with dread, have no fear. Many will want to drive this themselves. Personal growth is just that - *personal*. There's no one-size-fits-all you need to apply to everyone you employ.

Those with a keen interest in this area will explore on a regular basis some very clear ideas of where and how they want to grow, irrespective of what you do as a business. While you will find that this level of motivation to learn varies across your business, even those that don't devour every book they can get their hands on or aren't the first to sign up for every course that pops up on their Instagram feed, will still welcome some guidance in this area.

When it comes to your team members, they all want to evolve, consciously or not.

I've always believed that personal growth at work is driven by the individual and supported by the business. You should never be solely responsible for every aspect of someone's growth and development but you should support them by creating an open environment and allowing them opportunities wherever you can.

This may mean a bit more encouragement of those of your team who seem less outwardly keen on their own development to help them move forward and take ownership. For those who are so heavily invested in their own personal development that they take the lead in it the whole time, it may mean more time considering how their growth aligns with what you and your business need, as opposed to being weighted solely towards their specific goals.

Managing personal growth in your business, therefore, is about finding the point where someone's personal growth aspirations intersect with what the business needs from them. It is the sweet spot that will help you both to grow and where motivation will be at its peak.

For this to happen, of course, you need to get clear on what you need from them, as much as where they want to go.

Mind the Gap

A short-term way of identifying this sweet spot for growth is to look at both the responsibilities someone has and where you want their time and effort to be focused: you can find these in their job description if they have one and in their goals or expectations that you've set for them. They might be in any of the following areas:

1. **Business skills:** What skills do you need to have within the business which ensure you function and allow you to meet your goals? What product knowledge do people need to function effectively? These could be every person knowing what your core policies are right through to product and systems knowledge.
2. **Functional/Technical skills:** What skills do every team or role need to have to ensure competence? This is far-reaching across every area of your business, from ensuring you have the right amount of technology skills to ensuring you can sell effectively or manage the finances of the business.

3. **Personal skills:** Conflict management, communication, etc. are otherwise known as 'soft skills'. Despite the 'softness' of these skills, most of the nightmare issues that we come across in businesses stem from a distinct lack of these.
4. **Management and Leadership skills:** These are still 'personal' but are more specifically about how people behave when they hire, manage and grow your team. No-one is born a leader and as people progress into looking after others, they need the skills, practice and support to be able to do this effectively.

Whilst they are likely to hit some of these goals and responsibilities just by being reasonably diligent in their work and applying the skills they already have, there should be some areas which pop out as a bit of a stretch for them.

We call these areas 'skills gaps'.

You can identify these skills gaps in a number of ways: through feedback from others, performance reviews and results, through a skills gap analysis or, in many cases, just by observing them in their work.

Sometimes an individual may be well aware of what these gaps are, but using some of the more balanced methods of identifying these can help raise self-awareness about their areas of strength, their blindspots and the gaps that need closing. Feedback from those an individual has worked with *(clients, suppliers, other team members, etc.*

in what is known as '360 feedback') is particularly helpful. The more you do this in a positive way and encourage them to seek this feedback for themselves, the more you bake growth into your culture of 'how we do things' here.

Conducting a skills gap analysis is also useful, as it typically involves a self-assessment of key skills in addition to the feedback of others. Their involvement in the process can reduce a person's defensiveness and help balance out the feedback. You summarise the key skills someone needs in their role or to meet their goals and have both the individual and their manager score where they are, to see where the gaps fall between them. This simple process structures a development discussion and allows your team members to 'own' the areas they need to grow in, as well as see why they are important to the job.

Once spotted, these gaps can be reviewed on a regular basis to check progress and encourage motivation in the right direction.

Levelling up

As your team grows in confidence and becomes more skilled in their roles, they will look for advancement opportunities within the business, something that can cause you angst if you don't see a whole lot of open roles in your business. This doesn't mean you need to be able to guarantee anyone a promotion a year, but instead to answer the question, *"Where can I go from here?"* It can be useful to have some sort of framework in place to guide their development towards what is possible and what is needed by you.

Sometimes these frameworks are called career paths, at other times competency frameworks or even skills maps. But whatever you choose to call them, the common denominator is that they spell out the ideal knowledge, skills and behaviours in a reasonable amount of detail that someone needs to demonstrate in order to be successful in the different roles and different levels as they progress and expand their impact in your business. You can use them when someone joins: *"Here are the core skills we expect at your level,"* and in recruitment: *"We've thought about your future."*

Frameworks work well when you are scaling your business too. You can divide out the different needs you have in order to hit your short- and long-term goals as well as to show what you expect from every different level of role you have. When you're growing quite rapidly, you may also want to have different paths for different functions in your team to make it more personalised for team members: *e.g. development, sales, finance, etc.*

Once considered the preserve of large corporations and consulting firms and therefore something start-ups would hesitate to go near, in recent years, companies such as Monzo, Gitlab and Dropbox have shared their own versions of these career frameworks and how they've helped them scale. This disclosure has increased their popularity and encouraged many other businesses we know to create their own slightly simplified versions.

One such client of ours who has used skills maps to great effect is an advertising agency we've worked with for many years. They had grown from ten to forty people over a couple of years. Initially everyone was learning on the job and picking up new things each day but they then reached the stage where they were struggling to communicate how they saw people's development and what they could offer on a more long-term basis. The framework we jointly created allowed the whole team to see what skills were valued by the business and what impact they were expected to have as they progressed. They went on to look at how they could develop these. Everyone used them to focus their performance reviews on what and how they'd developed. In sharing these, conversations were prompted with people who felt their own career goals weren't aligned, in order to re-set. Potential exits were headed off before they happened.

Future You

Creating the space and time to discuss someone's future progress via one-to-ones or specific conversations about their development not only shows that you care about someone's long-term growth but also leads them to be even more focused and motivated to grow. We love it when other people take an interest in us and I've often found that a conversation about what 'Future You' looks like with your team members can be just the thing to strengthen your relationships with people and allow them to open up more about their own values and aspirations. The clearer the picture they communicate to you of where they imagine they will be – *whether as a leader in your business or something more functionally removed from it such as running their own vineyard in the South of France or learning to tap-dance* – the clearer you both become about what is possible in terms of the support you can provide.

One such business which looks beyond someone's growth linked to just their current role is *Cook*, a family-run B-Corp company based in my own neck of the woods. Over the last fifteen years, it has built its reputation on providing not just great 'home-cooked' frozen food, but on caring for those who work for and with them and investing in their personal development, with the emphasis firmly on the personal. Each year, they offer up a handful of places in their very own Dream Academy, a personal development programme with a difference. Whilst the aim is to bring their dreams to life, the key is that they can be either professional or personal. From losing weight to even moving jobs *(something many would view as an atypical approach and one to possibly avoid),* those who apply to join the academy can include any kind of goals they want. Once submitted, a lucky few are then chosen to have these dreams fulfilled with a mixture of financial and other tangible support. Over the years they've catered for many employees' desires, helped along by their own personal coach they call the Dream Manager. *Now there's a job title I'd like to have on my CV!*

Some of you may feel that putting your company's resources and time behind development that has little relevance to your business is not something you'd want to consider. However, the process of planning this personal development is something everyone should be encouraged to do. Typically, you do this by prompting someone to clarify their own personal development goals through a set of questions and then summarising them in a Personal Development Plan (PDP): a live document that your team member owns and in which they can keep track of their own progress. Even if they do end up including some goals outside the scope of what any business can really provide, the whole process of self-reflection can help people not only visualise what their future might look like but also start creating the building blocks to make it happen.

I think I was in my mid-twenties when, encouraged by my manager, I first wrote my first PDP. I'd never come across them before but I remember popping down a long list of 'wants', discussing it with him and agreeing on a few things that he would support me in. Since then, I've added to and amended it digitally. However, as I was writing this book, I dug out the original hard copy to see how it had held up longer term. Fully expecting to see a list of things that had been cast by the wayside, I was pleasantly surprised to see that out of the goals that included the more traditional 'getting my CIPD qualification' right through to 'becoming an HR Director' and (the moon-shot one) 'swimming the English Channel', I'd achieved a good 80 percent of them in the rough time frames I'd written down. It was a good reminder of the discussions and support my manager had provided at the time as well as the benefits that this process brought me in terms of my focus.

And of course, I can always swim the channel next year...

Growing pains don't have to be painful

Good intentions and development goals are brilliant of course, but to realise growth, some action needs to happen.

If you're in start-up mode, chances are you don't even need to think about how the growth will occur as it will do so naturally: after all, if you are working side by side, hearing what others are doing all around you, the effort to acquire individual knowledge feels minimal and just 'happens'.

Only the other day, I was introduced to someone who demonstrated stellar sales skills and an aptitude to command a room, yet her experience was much more traditionally 'back office'. When I complimented her and asked how she had crafted her skills so much so that she could probably train others in this regard, she thanked me and explained that she learnt them from, "*sitting next to our sales director in my last company for four years. Basically, I copied a lot of what I heard and it turns out – it works!*"

Whether it's sales, marketing or tech, the chances are that if you're in a smaller team sitting near each other, you can consider it to be the equivalent of taking a micro-MBA. *What marketing campaigns are we delivering? Which ones are working? What issues are your customers most annoyed at having?*

'Unconscious competence' I believe is its official term.

As your company expands, although there is less of an assumption that your team is developing at the same rate, learning can feel like it always gets put on the back burner, particularly when budgets and time are both tight and there are so many other pain points that feel more urgent kicking around on your to-do list.

But growing pains don't have to be painful.

The 70/20/10 model of learning (McCall, Lombardo and Eichinger) [4], named after their research conducted in 1996 into the most effective ways people learn, found that learning typically takes place in the following 'buckets':

- 70 percent takes place on the job for most people, perhaps learning how to do your existing job better and seeing how others do it.
- 20 percent takes place with others, either shadowing or working alongside them to see how they do things.
- 10 percent takes place formally, perhaps on training courses.

Despite some of the challenges to the exact ‘science’ of this model *(its origins are survey-based with a minimal range of those surveyed and some argue you can’t apply this prescriptively to an organisation either),* this model of learning has always resonated with me. Maybe that’s because it is less prescriptive in nature than many models, but also because I have had so many discussions with people about their growth in which it became apparent that what they were really talking about was just training. Both this research and my own experience is that 90 percent of people’s development is not about going on a training course.

I’m going to repeat it to emphasise the importance of this fact: 90 percent of people’s development is not about going on a training course. And if we’re being honest, in many cases *(depending on what stage of their career someone is at)*, 10 percent is pretty generous.

Instead of focusing on what training you can provide, start by encouraging people to trial different things in their roles. Can they research an area they’re interested in and apply it to their next marketing campaign? Can they interview customers and feed into your product team? Can they spot a topic which has come up through speaking with one of your customers or team and present something about it at the next company meeting?

Shadowing colleagues, joining others on sales calls, being part of another team's meeting or simply finding out more about a certain topic and trying to apply it to their own work are all examples of on-the-job learning, which will not only make the most of your budget but will also support the cornerstone of growth, that of continuous learning.

ABL

Way back when, as one of my projects for my CIPD studies, I chose the topic of Peter Senge's theory of the 'Learning Organisation'. [5]

Senge is less popularly referenced in recent times, although I feel sure his time in the sun will come again. The core principles of his book, *The Fifth Discipline*, are as relevant today as they were when it was published in 1990. Senge was a scientist by trade and proposed that all businesses should seek to become a Learning Organisation in order to receive a massive boost to their creativity and adaptability.

His theory suggested five key pillars of organisational processes – *personal mastery, mental models, building shared vision, team learning and systems thinking* – that his readers should include in their business, which they should keep reviewing on a regular and continuous basis.

Whilst it's true that there are complexities to this model in terms of assessing how these five processes work together as a system, my research of the topic, its application in business and my general experience over the years have led me to prefer a greatly simplified version: Always Be Learning (ABL).

With ABL, the emphasis is on involving your teams themselves in communication and continuous learning as well as the practices and processes you use in the business. Ask questions like: *How often do I have my team meetings? Do I give the team a chance to let me know what they're thinking? What reviews do I have in place to capture the learning from any project, sale or initiative? How do I capture feedback from all those involved?*

ABL saw one of our clients bag the number two slot for Learning and Development in the Best Small Companies [6] to work for in recent years, the first time they were surveyed, despite never having had a formal learning 'policy' or 'budget' in their company. The Best Companies process surveys key areas of engagement in organisations by asking employees directly what their views are. Given the number of small companies in the UK stands at over five million in any given year, it's the most competitive category.

How did they manage this? Regardless of their formal policies (or lack of them), learning is core to what they believe. They thought about it at every step of their journey and built it into 'how they operated'. This included reflecting on all the experiences they'd learned from to date and thinking about what they could do differently, as well as encouraging people to try new things all the time. One example was doing away with email as the default communication mode and switching to an internal social media platform, on which everyone was encouraged to ask questions and share information with a transparency-first approach. Of course, this didn't mean people couldn't message each other directly or their clients couldn't still communicate with them via email. It meant that a lot of the learning typically done in a start-up (when everyone involved is in the same room) took place online instead: a mix of Senge's Learning Organisation principles and the 70/20/10 learning models.

When we bake our learning into our internal experiences, the added bonus is that it recognises another 'B' word, an important one in any business owner's vocab.

I'm talking of course about the Budget.

Cash flow and grow positive

Much of the advice in this book does not really have a financial outlay attached to it: there's no cost in creating meaningful work for people or letting them know how much you value them.

Supporting growth is not expensive. In fact, *not* supporting growth is expensive for your business, but training is a different thing.

Once upon a time in a land filled with grey suits and Blackberrys, I was responsible for a considerable amount of money on the training line of the annual budget. Rather, I had a considerable amount of budget on the training line in a transitory capacity between months one and three of every financial year. Come months four to six, however, it was a different story. Every single year I can remember, the questions came: *"Do we really need security training?" and "Do you think we could maybe defer the leadership coaching?"* Every. Single. Year. Without fail. This line was pared down so much in the end, in the same way, in every company I worked in, that I have become convinced over time that in accounting and finance 'school', it is taught as a line to 'hide' things in if they want some buffering!

Since those heady days spent in a corporate world, I've never had a flush budget to support the development of my team. In fact, I've never really had a budget for it in any start-up I've worked in. And when I have, I've had to fight for every proposal I felt would pay dividends.

Although you also know that your budgets don't swell as you move from start-up to toddler and into teenager in your business (even with an injection of cash at various stages I have rarely seen 'we need money to invest in training' as a core part of any investor deck), as I write this during the cost-of-living crisis of 2023, money has never seemed tighter. The ability to think creatively and ABL have never felt so relevant.

Cash flow positive practices I've seen to great effect therefore include:

1. **The 'f' word:** Yes, you can and should provide feedback to everyone in the business and the more regular it is the better. It's free, it's motivating and it's one of the main ways people will grow. Instant feedback is good – it is so much easier to say it in the moment and although we have to get ahead of ourselves and (for those of us who are 'British') get over the cultural barrier of not wanting to say anything too personal, it's invaluable to people.
2. **The errors of our ways:** We learn from our mistakes. Accept that people will make them and when they are, don't come down hard on the person. After all, we have all learned and grown as a result of our finest mess-ups!
3. **Special projects:** Is there something you could really do with help with but don't feel you've got someone in 'that' team who can? Ask around to see if anyone can help you and is prepared to give it a go. As someone who's done everything from debt collection and marketing prior to and parallel to my career in HR and People, I've learned a lot from the more random projects I've been part of.
4. **Onboarding questions:** People are often most open about what they want to achieve when they have just joined. Whilst not everyone might have a five-year plan, you can certainly find out what growth spurts people have had previously by using a survey, which can help eliminate some of the guesswork.

5. **Learning from others:** Your team will have lots of knowledge they can share and will be happy to share. From learning how to cultivate different types of mindset to specific technical workshops, we've seen internal learning sessions used to great effect. Part of the learning someone gets is from preparing such a session.

And there are many more. *(See, I didn't even talk about training courses!)*

Your Action:

1. Hold 'stay' interviews with key employees to understand what keeps them with you and what keeps them growing.
2. Undertake a quick skills gap analysis to understand what skills you will need in your business and what you currently have.
3. Encourage Personal Development through people's own PDPs and finding the 'sweet spot' between what they're after and what you want.
4. Start building a career framework of core skills which you consider to be key to your business and let people know what you expect at each level. This helps answer the question, "Where can I go next?"
5. Always Be Learning: from each other, from projects you've undertaken and from feedback you get from your customers, partners and each other.

[1] Grandview Research, 2022, *Personal Development Market Size*
[2] Statista.com, 2022, *Market Size of Personal Training Industry*
[3] Professor Teresa Amabile and Steven Kramer, 2011, *The Progress Principle: Using Small Wins to Ignite Joy, Engagement, and Creativity at Work.*
[4] McCall, Lombardo and Eichinger, *70/20/10 model of learning*
[5] Senge, *The Fifth Discipline: The Art and Practice of the Learning Organization* (1990, rev. 2006)
[6] *Best Companies, Best Small Companies Awards*

6
Inclusion

Despite the great plans you have in place and what the illustrative charts of your ideal sales forecasts may show, the path of growth will never be linear. It will always be one of continuous and iterative improvement. We grow, we adapt, we reflect and then we grow some more.

This cycle brings you not just more self-awareness of your own needs and strengths but makes you more aware of the strengths in others and the fact that including them in your journey will help your growth: seek out people whose strengths balance your own views and experiences.

It also brings us to our next principle which helps you create the MAGIC in your team: that of Inclusion.

We're All in This Together

At its most basic level, an Inclusive business is one where everyone feels welcomed, valued and safe. People's ideas and contributions are considered. People feel 'at home' enough with you to bring their true selves to work and be comfortable sharing these with you. There are many components to being inclusive and lots of reasons why the principle of Inclusion should resonate, but given that it is most commonly seen as going hand in hand with Diversity, it makes sense to start with this.

Diversity and Inclusion. They're similar, but not the same-same.

Diversity can be characterised as respect for and celebration of the differences we have. Strong levels of this in your business means having a team with a range of backgrounds, experiences and views that are not only different from your own but which represent our society as a whole. Typically speaking, however, many businesses simply translate this into a need to focus on sex, sexual orientation, disability and race making sure that there is adequate representation of those who possess different characteristics related to these groups.

This in part comes from the legislation that protects specific groups of people from discrimination in the workplace. That includes those with the aforementioned characteristics as well as additional ones in the UK including age, maternity and pregnancy, gender reassignment, religion and marital status. These, of course, are groups which have a good reason to be protected from discrimination in life as well as work: after all, they are groups which have been most underrepresented in the workplace compared to their makeup in society for years. Recent research in 2021 [1] found that 76 percent of those classified as White ethnicity were employed, compared with 67 percent of people from all other ethnic groups combined (GOV.UK - Ethnicity Facts and Figures); women make up 51 percent of our population (GOV.UK - 2021 Census) [2] yet only 42 percent of all workers. And those with disabilities fare even worse, with an employment rate of 52.7 percent compared to 81 percent for non-disabled people (GOV.UK). [3]

Removing discrimination is therefore an absolute 'given' in any business. But a much more positive aim would be to understand the contributions that these different perspectives can make to your business and to include more of them. And we could go further than the nine protected characteristics *(it's not a phrase that trips off the tongue easily, is it?)*, as our world is much more varied than that, not least in the way we think (neurodiversity) and in how we have grown up (socio-economic differences).

In life, we don't hang out with people who are all the same as us, so why would we at work? We know instinctively that this would make life a bit boring *at the very least*. It's the same in our business.

In the last five years alone, neurodiversity - a term coined by Judy Singer and which describes a variation in cognitive patterns of individuals - has become much more commonly recognised and understood. It is estimated that

15 percent of our population would be considered neurodiverse, across a broad spectrum of diagnoses, ADHD, ASD, etc., often with multiple concurrent diagnoses. Recognition helps, of course, in starting to think about the value these different ways of thinking can bring to businesses, but – *right now at least* – it doesn't necessarily translate into reflections in employment figures. According to the UK's National Autistic Society [4], only 16 percent of autistic adults in the UK are in full-time employment, compared to 47 percent of non-disabled people.

Similarly, recognising socio-economic factors as ones to consider when it comes to diversity of thought, including where people went to school and what income level their parents had, is also an area that has come to prominence in recent years. The term *Old Boys' Network* is used to summarise our understanding that some members of society benefit disproportionately in the workplace over others, such as those who come from private schools and privileged backgrounds. And that's even before you look at the solid data. Once you add this in, the picture becomes an ever more stark reminder of the influence of socio-economics on the roles of power people end up having in the workplace and the limited perspectives this can bring with it: with only approximately seven percent of the country educated via private schooling, 71 percent of barristers, 27 percent of CEOs and 29 percent of our House of Commons are made up of those who did the same, as found by the Social Equality Commission [5]

When you're looking to design and enhance your team with diversity in mind, don't just think of the numbers or percentages: they are the starting point. It is a little like calorie counting without a thought for the nutritional value of the food you're putting into your body. Solely thinking of having X percent of any demographic on a list without considering everyone's contribution seems to be rather missing the point of the value greater diversity can bring.

It is definitely a building block towards inclusion, but not the full picture.

Many businesses have understood for a long time that in theory diversity and inclusion are important to have in their companies which will benefit them, yet have not always been intentional about taking action to make it happen. Events of the last few years have accelerated changes to these ways of thinking, however. Due in part to the sets of circumstances that gave rise to the MeToo movement and George Floyd's murder in 2020 (to name just two of the major headline events), diversity and inclusion were thrust into the global spotlight in a way that no-one could ignore.

Anyone running a business in mid-2020 when Floyd died may well recall navigating various conversations with their team around race and ethnicity in the workplace: for some, this was the first time they had discussed the topic at work. The conversations varied in type and intensity, but the most vocal participants came from groups who were underrepresented and often felt marginalised, and they came with a significant level of frustration. Many business owners I spoke with felt taken aback by these frank conversations and, let's face it, slightly unprepared, but many stepped up nevertheless and did a lot of listening to understand why their teams were feeling the way they were. Once the shock of the events themselves and (for some) the initial reaction to the events had settled and there was time to digest the feedback received, many were left in no doubt of the strength of feeling that had been shared about certain issues: a general lack of proactive inclusion and a lack of consideration were just two that many people of colour shared in the conversations I was aware of.

If the feelings shared post-Floyd's murder were a tsunami of brutal honesty, then the earlier swells had been seen in businesses in the years prior to this, as the MeToo movement gathered momentum. Initially used as a term by Tarana Burke to empower women who had been sexually assaulted, particularly those who were women of colour or young or otherwise vulnerable, it gained traction online in 2016 and morphed into a much broader wave of awareness and discussion about how unfairly women were treated in society after a tweet invited people to respond 'me too' [6] if they'd ever experienced sexual harassment at work. The responses were quick and significant in numbers and, emboldened by the transparency in experiences shared by others, women right, left and centre came forward with tales of harassment, misogyny and other detrimental treatment at work, discussing this offline at their places of work as well as online and making no secret of how they felt practices needed to change.

Those affected by these events grew braver during these times in challenging what they saw and felt as behaviour and practices which had bias in race or sex. Horrendous as it is to think that crimes took place in order for these topics to be front and centre in business, there is no doubt in my mind about their significance in accelerating the growth of more positive practices in diversity and inclusion in the workplace, as the impact and repercussions of these events were felt around the globe, regardless of where you called home.

Whether they were demonstrating on the streets in Boston, Massachusetts, or simply sitting talking to their manager about their concerns in Boston, Lincolnshire, people's conversations during these times weren't empty complaints, but people expressing their frustration of wanting to be included.

Remember how I mentioned in the Meaning *chapter that the common denominator amongst people interviewing for a new job was that they wanted 'to be part of something'?* It's the 'part of' that we're talking about here, rather than the 'something'.

Inclusion in this sense, therefore, is not about paying lip service to diversity and making sure you've got people in your team representative of any *(or all)* of the characteristics protected by law. It is about understanding and making sure *everyone* in your business gets a chance to be 'part of' it.

Because there's no point, of course, in having a wealth of experience in your team if you're not able to draw from it. Sure, it may look good on a couple of sales slides and/or your website to show the breadth of experiences and the demographics of your team, but it won't reap all the many, many benefits on offer.

Boxes ticked? Maybe. *But sparks lit?* Definitely not.

Can't put a price on inclusion?

Quite aside from feeling like you should look at inclusion as a principle because everyone's talking about it, having greater representation has been shown to make better business. *And who wouldn't want that?*

We all know how tricky it is to attract the right talent into your business, but you're much more likely to do so if you have a greater culture of inclusion and people can have their say. A recent survey found that 69 percent of Gen Z job seekers would 'absolutely' be more likely to apply to a role where there was an ethnically and racially diverse workforce (Tallo, Gen Z Demands Diversity and Inclusion Strategy 2020) [7] and we know that people align with businesses and brands that share the same values.

When it comes to this issue, therefore, the people appear to have spoken.

Likewise, when it comes to company output and the stuff which really gives your shareholders something to highlight in their annual report, the research into the impact on your bottom line is also pretty compelling: in 2018, a survey by Boston Consulting Group [8] found that companies with greater diversity at management level produced 19 percent better revenue for their products and services than those without. Moreover, in 2018 McKinsey [9] released the third paper in their series on diversity which showed that companies with greater ethnic and cultural diversity outperform those who lack it by up to 33 percent.

For the average UK SME with an estimated profit of £300k (Statista) [10] that could be a whole lot of £££ you're leaving on the table.

Getting these kinds of specific hard metrics on the impact of inclusion if you're a smaller business is tricky as most just don't have that size of data set. However, even if you can't measure in pure ££ immediately, and you're just thinking of all the areas that build towards a healthy balance sheet and strong company valuation - *engagement of teams, ideas and innovation, increased well-being and reduced stress for you (and everyone else)* - these can all be linked to increased inclusion.

Of course, you may not be looking to sell your business or be remotely interested in receiving investment, but you are keen to be successful. As someone much wiser than me explained many years ago, all the things that make a business valuable for sale or investment are also the things which will be good for your bottom line.

Sales and new business will be a key area where you see this first. And for any of you who pitch for any organisation involved with public funds, you already know that a part of your proposal needs to include information on the diversity of your firm, something becoming much more common in private businesses too. One business I worked with many years ago was rapped on the metaphorical knuckles by more than one prospective client due to their pitch deck being full of a team who were 'pale, male and stale', an effect made worse by the fact that they were wearing identical clothes in their pictures. Their team was one hundred percent homogenous. Even ten-plus years ago, this was not a good look.

Cranking up the ideas machine

I can't imagine there are many reading this book who haven't had their own experiences of using Amazon Prime and its glorious One-Click system. It is responsible for many a scratched head *("Why the hell did I order that last night?")*, a slightly scared delivery man *(our dog's bark is far worse than his bite)* and a fair few arguments if it comes out of a joint account. It is all of these things because its ease of use leads us to spend considerably more on Amazon than we perhaps would otherwise, something that only further lines the pockets of Jeff Bezos.

But did he have the idea for the One-Click system himself? *Did he Jeff!*

It is true that he set the direction in terms of wanting to make the ordering process simpler for customers; however, it was one of Amazon's employees who came up with the idea and who designed the software which allowed the One-Click system to take shape. This is a prime (pun fully intended) example of the power of employee-led initiatives that, in this case, was termed a 'game changer' in the e-commerce world and which boosted the already significant profits of Amazon.

Ditto the Happy Meal: invented by Dick Brams, a McDonald's employee in St. Louis who saw the potential to attract more families to the restaurants by packaging fast-food happiness in brightly coloured boxes which sell by the million.

Whilst you may not think your business needs something on the scale of Amazon Prime or millions of *'can I get one of those, Mum?'*, innovation is a strong pillar of success for any business, from meeting room names to product ideas that have increased your client offerings. The more inclusive you are, the easier it is to crank up the ideas machine on a regular and long-term basis.

After all, when you've got so much on your plate yet think you alone have the answers to your problems, not only is it hard to see things clearly, but you're also restricting your perspective. No matter how creative you are, this will always limit you.

Different perspectives come from different lived experiences, so if we work in a homogenous world, we'll never spot these things.

I've worked in plenty of businesses where it's the employees who have come up with the ideas to further the business, some of which have been taken up and others receive a 'thank you for the suggestion but not this time'. Wherever I've seen this level of contribution, a strong degree of what is known as 'psychological safety' has also been present.

This term was first coined by Carl Rogers, a clinical psychologist in the 1950s, subsequently made more famous in the last ten years by Professor Amy Edmonson. It is used to describe a state at work where you have the belief that you won't be punished or humiliated for speaking up with ideas, questions, concerns, or mistakes, and that you can challenge constructively. It is one of the most important concepts in your relationship with your team members in general, and it's impossible to have lots of innovation without lots of psychological safety.

Ideas rarely arrive fully formed. Instead, innovation comes from testing, sharing and building on previous learnings, typically involving more than one person. If you don't allow for these mistakes and learnings to happen and you don't welcome ideas from all quarters, you're never likely to see a queue of them forming from your team ever again.

Even Han Solo needed more

Perhaps you consider yourself to be a bit more 'Han Solo' than group decision-maker. (Note that I steered away from the 'control freak' phrase!) If so, then it's worth considering that including others doesn't just give you different viewpoints to spot the things you may have missed, but it also helps take the load off you to get more done and makes things a little less lonely.

One of my longtime clients, David, was growing his business exceptionally well. In the first year, all growth targets were hit, his team's growth was on track and he'd just closed his seed round of funding. All looked rosy, except that David was anything but when you spoke with him. In fact, David was the grumpiest person alive when I would catch up with him: short-tempered, berating others and constantly complaining about how everyone wasn't pulling their weight in the business. When I tentatively asked how he delegated his work and if there was anything I could help with, the answer was always a version of, *"No, it's just quicker if I do it myself," or, "If I tell them what to do, it never gets done right."* Ring any bells, anyone?

This was a cycle that showed no signs of being broken: the more there was to do, the more he took on and the less time he had to delegate to others or include them, meaning he had even less time to do things and he excluded them further. Despite considerable resilience and wellness in other areas of this person's life, burnout would be his next stop if he didn't change course.

Into the mix at the same time came the fact that he had lost a couple of key members of the team: fed up with being excluded from some of the decisions over the future of the business and feeling like their suggestions didn't particularly matter *(Hello, Chapter 2?)*, they voted with their feet and left, only adding to this downward spiral.

Fortunately, he recognised that things couldn't continue as they were. A plan was put in place to reduce his workload by delegating to a mix of his management team plus others in the company. He opened up to others in his team about how difficult this part of the growth cycle was and the offers to help came flooding forward thick and fast. It wasn't easy – a considerable amount of time was still invested in coaching to overcome the fear of 'it's all on me' to effectively delegate and trust others – but it started to pay dividends.

Many of us have been in this situation too: we've had so much on our plates that the tension in our heads just grows and grows. Whilst there are lots of things that perhaps do end up with you as the final signatory or decision maker, including others will make getting to that point a darn sight easier, even if it feels like it's not the 'easy' choice.

You've heard the phrase: *'A problem shared is a problem halved'*? The same holds true whether it's a problem or an item on your to-do list so do yourself a favour and let others in or simply spell out that you can't manage this on your own and you're asking for help.

Han Solo, after all, needed more than just Chewbacca to defeat the Dark Side. He needed the whole of the rebel alliance.

NFI can damage your health

It's not just *your* stress levels and health that can be given a boost by inclusion, because you want your team to be happy and healthy too. That means allowing them to play their part.

In most of the *(many hundreds)* of employee surveys I've ever done to check engagement levels in various businesses, 'communication' always comes out as an area in which people want more, no matter what company I'm looking at: from one that's very progressive to one where they feel they have 'a lot of issues'. *The reason?* We all want to know what's going on.

This means being an active part of something.

This need for social inclusion is something we all have naturally programmed into our chemistry and is governed by the hormone oxytocin, which also promotes trust.

Remember 'that' party you were Not F****** Invited *(NFI) to?* Remember how even if you didn't necessarily want to go, the fact that others were invited and you weren't, meant that you felt just a little bit peeved? This is your instinct talking. It is sounding the inner alarm bell when you're excluded from situations. It's a fear of social exclusion that we all share to different degrees.

This is why we get uneasy when we're separated from our friends and family (think Covid), why your team feel more positive when they're included in discussions about where to go on your team day out, and why we're peeved if we're NFIed to the meeting to discuss the changes being made to any processes that we're part of.

It might seem like it is small things that influence this: an oversight or an error that means someone has been dropped off the invite list. However, over the last few years I've investigated a hefty number of grievances that people have raised in their teams which include people citing '*not being invited to meetings*' as a very real source of their perception that they're being treated unfairly.

Perception = individual reality. Even if someone feels slighted in error rather than by intent, this still has an impact on people which is only reversed when consistent inclusion has happened.

Some people, of course, will not complain or raise concerns if they feel they're excluded, they'll just slowly withdraw into themselves. This is dangerous to them and your business. For them, research has shown that exclusion impacts people's health in a negative way if these feelings are left unresolved. When people feel constantly rejected, it leads to problems including anxiety and high blood pressure. Whilst it's obviously not as simple as saying that missing someone off an invite list on a one-off occasion will send them straight to the doctor, if you do not involve others in what is going on in the business, the effective correlation between individual health and inclusion is clear.

The impact is felt in your business too. The phrase 'quiet quitting' has sprung up this year, used to define a state where people do the bare minimum they can in their jobs to avoid being fired. It's where people have the exact opposite state of creating the MAGIC we are talking about in this book; rather than let their mental health suffer, they withdraw on a very basic level to protect themselves.

All of this can come at a cost.

We're only human

This is all well and good, but as you no doubt found out when you started on the journey to becoming more inclusive in all areas of your business, it doesn't always go to plan. Our brains aren't always fully up to date with our intentions and sometimes things get in the way. Ourselves mainly.

If you have a brain, you have bias.

Our biases are decisions or judgements we make on the basis of our own experiences and influences. Most are made faster than the speed of light and most are unconscious, having been built up through early socialisation, upbringing and media influences. They help us separate groups of information and – *when it comes to people* – categorise them based on various characteristics and what we associate with those. Because they're so deeply rooted, it's possible that even if you have only positive motives, bias can still show up when it's not invited.

Whenever I'm running training for businesses on this topic, I always use a self-confessed example of my own unconscious bias highlighted by the Harvard Implicit Association Tests. [11] These tests were developed by a group of professors in 1998 and are available for anyone to take online. They are designed to show your attitudes and beliefs, particularly in areas you may not have ever checked before. You can test your beliefs on a range of topics, from your opinion on race to age to gender and even weight. I have taken a few tests; I was pretty amazed to find that one showed a slightly negative bias against older workers. Not a big one, but a bias nonetheless. Given that (in employment terms and particularly in the tech world) anyone over forty is viewed as an older worker, I was staggered to realise that this may mean I have a bias against myself!

As I have discovered, I'm definitely not the only person to have some sort of bias around my own 'in group'. In fact, even one of the professors who developed the test found the same. That doesn't mean you should lose sleep over it. It simply means that no matter how good your intentions are about how you treat people, we all carry perceptions of groups from our upbringing and experiences as shown to us by the media, our social groups, and role models - basically everything that influenced you growing up - that are still retained by our brains. After all, we're only human.

Becoming aware of them first, therefore, is an admirable step towards working out how you can mitigate them, so try learning about your own and challenge others on theirs.

I just hire the best person for the job

It doesn't come easily, of course. Bias can feel like a bit of a dirty word sometimes. "I don't have any biases," I've often heard said, or, "I just hire the best person for the job."

The reasons these statements don't exactly go hand in hand are: a) there's nothing unusual or awful about having bias, it's just fact; b) As we don't know what they all are, how on earth do we know if they affect our ability to hire? After all, as we've just mentioned, most are unconscious.

Part of the reason underrepresented groups in the workplace are underrepresented in the first place can be down to bias and how these show up in the core processes: how we hire people, develop people and generally treat them. No-one intentionally says they want to hire people with certain characteristics or exclude others, yet it keeps happening.

All in all, it appears that affinity bias *(where we tend to connect with or prefer people with similar backgrounds and experiences to our own)* is one of the most present biases in our recruitment processes. This was shown in 2019 when Nuffield College [12] undertook a study in the UK and found that those who came from minority ethnic backgrounds had to send 60 percent more CVs (or 80 percent when it came to those of Nigerian origin) than their white counterparts to get an interview. The study also found that this hadn't changed much since the 1960s.

Ditto when it comes to Gender: in 2012, a study by Proceedings of the National Academy of Sciences [13] found that both men and women *(remember what I said about bias against your own in-groups?)* rated more men than women hireable and furthermore assigned them higher salary levels when determining what they should be paid.

Despite just wanting to hire the best person for the job, we clearly need a helping hand when it comes to actually doing this.

Shortly after starting their business, one of our clients realised they were in danger of following the path of all of their competitors in having a male-heavy team and wanted to consciously diversify. In their industry, there is a leaning towards men making up the majority of employees and if people hire solely on experience, then it can become a self-perpetuating cycle. *Their solution?* They tore up the rule book and started afresh with their recruitment processes. No more CVs used for hiring and instead just a simple request to their applicants: download the software they were going to be working on and 'have a go' at creating something with it to share. This gave everyone the same chance to access the process as the evaluation criteria instantly shifted to effort and creativity, rather than the more traditional route of whether you got a 2:1 qualification or went to a red-brick university. It was a novel way to hire and run the recruitment process, ironing out a lot of the bias built into the CV screening process and producing some staggering results. Within two years of this strategy, their employee base split was 55/45 percent male/female - a significant improvement compared with their competitors in their industry.

I'm not remotely biased

Even when the evidence for affinity bias is significant, one area I'm fairly sure will never make any protected list but which is important when it comes to diversity is location bias.

Since Covid, we have a divide that will not be solved easily: those that come into the office and those who would prefer to stay at home and work. Each side has different arguments and many companies have gone down the mandatory route for some anyhow. My belief is that when someone is not in the 'physical' room, it is easier for people to exclude them.

For many who are now managing a hybrid situation or still have a lot of people online, it can make communication just that little bit harder as everything needs to be just that little bit more intentional. Rotating people in the 'chair' during online calls, asking people to make sure they have their cameras on, sending people agendas in advance: all of these can be used to make sure people feel included.

After all, to truly feel a sense of belonging, we need to feel that our voice has been heard. And how hard is that when all it seems to be saying is, "You're on mute."?

Let's start at the very beginning

It has been mooted that businesses will soon be required to share statistics on the ethnicity of their teams publicly in an effort to raise awareness. However, this has yet to come into play. Currently, the only reporting businesses must provide is on Gender, and only for those with more than two hundred and fifty people. Although progressive businesses typically provide more information to be as transparent as possible, there is no law forcing businesses to consider it.

To make this the norm in your business and to drive all of the high performance and benefits and other goodies that come with diversity, you need to challenge yourself to make this a part of things.

One of our clients publishes an annual update on their efforts towards making their business more diverse and inclusive despite there being no need for them to do so: the changes to practices they've made, the results of internal surveys they've held and any other relevant actions. They recognise that in their community, people – stakeholders, clients, employees – all care that they are being clear on their intentions. Whilst in some years their progress seems to be slower than others, it's recognised that it will be iterative.

Another client of mine has made a very public goal to have a more equal gender split in their teams within eighteen months: a tall order if you're only twenty people and are currently far from that. But in making it public, they've set the bar har that this is what the CEO wants, leaving the team no room for ambiguity in what they value.

It's tough, of course, when you have low employee numbers and low turnover, as change may not come about as quickly as in other businesses. But as I said to the client when we were discussing how to make his all-white male leadership team more diverse and who had commented, *"What am I supposed to do, Claire, fire them all?"*,a good start is to verbally share with your team the very best of intentions to move towards a place of greater inclusivity and then keep reinforcing this. Can't change your leadership team? How about diversifying your board or getting additional advisers in, even if you don't have a formal 'board'? Whatever you can do to get additional voices in the room will help you achieve this.

The two main stages of your team's life cycle that often have the greatest influence on inclusion are within your recruitment and development cycles.

In line with your intentions therefore, I recommend looking at how you're attracting anyone to your business: your adverts, the agencies you're using and what you're saying in them and to them.

There are two bits of research often quoted when it comes to the application process for any role. The first is that when it comes to job adverts, a Hewlett-Packard internal survey found that women tend not to apply for roles unless they have all the qualifications listed on the job advert while men tend to apply if they have 60 percent of the qualifications.[14] The second finding is that there is such a thing as *gendered wording* when it comes to adverts or how we communicate. According to the research undertaken by Gaucher, Friesen and Kay *(Journal of Personality and Social Psychology, January 2011)* [15], this type of wording lays very subtle breadcrumbs in its language, with certain words appealing to one gender over another which therefore reduces the likelihood of the other applying. Some words such as 'competitive' and 'ambitious' are considered more agentic (and associated with male stereotypes) and appeal more to male readers, with some people less likely to feel they belong to those roles. Others such as ‘support’ and ‘develop’ are considered more communal (and associated with female stereotypes) and appeal to more female readers.

Do your job adverts use inclusive language? Do you have inclusive statements on any adverts? Are your partners (e.g. agencies) aware that you particularly encourage applications from underrepresented groups?

If it’s a ‘no’ to any or all of these things, you’ve got some great actions straight away.

With gender decoders available for free online [16], there's no excuse not to whizz your Job Descriptions (JDs) through one of them to see whether your wording is more attractive to a particular gender or another and needs more balance: it’s like getting a second and third set of eyes on them for free.

Likewise with your own website and adverts, you can use these spaces to communicate your inclusivity by shining a light on the fact that you particularly welcome applications from underrepresented groups (and then make sure your partners know this too). This is not to say that you’d prefer to hire more ‘women/ethnic minorities/less abled’ candidates *(that’s known as positive discrimination and is still illegal in the UK)* but that you ‘encourage applications from underrepresented groups’.

Moving through to the assessment stage, training anyone who is involved is a must. Interviewing is still the most common assessment process in the UK and I have had various conversations over the years with hiring managers which involve me challenging their 'data' gleaned from interviews. I have used phrases such as, *"Unfortunately, x person's experience of playing the guitar is* not *an indicator of them being able to do a good job for you."* These conversations have left me with the distinct impression that we are not natural truth seekers when it comes to such a process and left unchecked.....

This is mainly because it is hard and our brains seek the path of least resistance. It is hard enough that in any one interview you have the difficult job of selling the role, building rapport and assessing whether the person in front of us is going to do a good job - *all at the same time in a forty-minute period* - so when we add the need to overcome our own biases into the mix, we need something that's easy to implement. This juggling act sometimes leads to places where we find ourselves talking too much (a common downfall is that we can be as nervous as the candidate), not asking the right questions (see above re: guitar!) or worse still, making assumptions based on extremely limited information (step forward your biases).

People are always amazed when we share in The HR Hub's recruitment training that even with the most robust assessment process you are only ever likely to have a 63 percent [17] chance of getting it right and predicted performance accurately. But with the right training on structured assessment methods and their scoring based on criteria which are 'evidenced' (not assumed), you can go a long way to getting close to that number. You need the structure to scale fast as well as to make your decisions more robust.

When opportunity knocks

Once in the door, however, one of the biggest complaints I've heard from employees (in even some of the most progressive businesses) regards inclusivity in terms of development. More specifically when people feel that opportunities for development don't come so readily.

This can be about knowing what training budget is available (and how to access it) right through to understanding what other opportunities there are in the business. And it doesn't need to be about new roles: sometimes it is related to how to get on new projects, work with new clients or do something slightly different. We all want a bit of variety and, as mentioned in Chapter 5, Growth: we all want to grow.

So when a new role comes along because someone leaves or a need is spotted, if someone is 'slotted into' the role without so much as a 'this is going to happen and this is why' to everyone else, it can leave a bit of a sour taste.

Of course, you may need new roles that you feel would not fit anyone's skills in the business. If that's the case, I urge you to be transparent about why that is, in order to head off any potential issues before they start: either disgruntlement amongst the current employees or pain for your new team member to sort out as their first task. Too many times I've seen business owners having to smooth down situations belatedly after they've forgotten to tell a team member that they won't be reporting to them anymore and that they will *'really like their new manager'*. If you're being introduced to your new manager on their first day, believe me when I say it doesn't feel much like inclusion.

People don't always want to move roles either. Sometimes they just want to know about them. So be frank about all the opportunities there may be for people and, where it's relevant, what budget goes hand in hand with the opportunity.

Sometimes that means having a tough conversation with someone, explaining why you might not think they're right for the role and allowing them the chance to have their say. You might want to avoid this as you don't want to hurt someone's feelings; however, they're going to be a lot more hurt if they feel they've been passed over and can't work out why. Transparency works best here.

We've talked about accountability already when it comes to performance. This is a chance to show yourself to be accountable and live up to the values you communicate.

Educating Rita *(and Pete, Sam and Daniel too...)*

It's on all of us as business owners to educate ourselves on areas which impact our world, including inclusivity. When it comes to your team, helping to educate them is the place to start rather than waiting to be educated in the first place by those who are underrepresented.

You may have already encouraged your team to start learning themselves by sharing a couple of well-placed blog posts on the topics or asking them to take their own implicit-bias tests to gain a bit of self-awareness. Training is an option too – *we've done many sessions with teams to open discussions and raise awareness* – however, a couple of our clients fund monthly speaker series for someone (occasionally someone in the public eye) to come and talk to their teams about their experiences. The budget version would be sharing curated TEDx or other online talks with your team. Whichever way the message of inclusivity is delivered, the element of storytelling lends itself very well to group sessions and makes it feel less like a 'lecture' than some training can be.

Whatever you choose to do, your team is much more likely to take note if you are involved, so lead by example and join any sessions booked.

I hear you

Where it all comes together, of course, is not just by giving the platform where everyone can contribute rather than having to ask about what is going on explicitly, but by listening to others about their experiences and showing that you've heard, in order to encourage more inclusivity.

Time and again I've seen business owners who want to understand what their teams 'really' feel by conducting a survey or three, but then ignore most of the results if they don't like the outcome!

Whilst anonymous surveys work quite well to uncover how people in a business feel about specific things, there will always be people who won't fill them out and after a while, a bit of survey lethargy kicks in which reduces the participation *(made worse if you don't acknowledge in the first place - see above).*

Several of my clients encourage this by just checking in with people to get their views - coffee chats by any other name. This is one way of doing it if you have a team small enough to get around all of them. Explaining what the goals are and making it into a bit of a game in which others can submit ideas to get around the challenges is another one. These do two things simultaneously: gather more insight from different perspectives and create a long list of ideas you can then share to implement.

Another way a client of mine has successfully promoted inclusion in their business is by creating a Reward Board: a cross-section of individuals in their business who can help to ensure that compensation is paid fairly to the teams and bring different voices to the discussions. There is always a framework that the business operates in and each person included understands that what they are discussing is confidential; however, the inclusion of those outside of the management team to discuss the principles of how compensation is decided helps inclusivity and builds a considerable amount of trust.

Another has an Employee Board (EB) which they work with to provide suggestions to solve various problems in the business as well as use as a sounding board to test out any 'soft launches' of changes they want to make to the business. The members of the EB rotate amongst the team to encourage even more inclusivity and it allows everyone to feel involved. In the past, I've seen some business owners get scared of this type of 'togetherness' as they feel they are letting too much control go, but most people want the best for you and your business and this should be embraced rather than feared.

Because at the end of the day, we really are all in this together.

Your Action:

1. Be intentional about involving others from the get-go.
2. Back up your intent by including people in decision-making.
3. Take your own tests to check on bias (and ask your team to do them too).
4. Make it clear that you welcome applications from underrepresented groups.
5. Keep track of and communicate the changes and progress you're making.

---

[1] *GOV.UK - Ethnicity Facts and Figures*, 2021
[2] *GOV.UK - 2021 Census*
[3] *GOV.UK*
[4] Autism.org.uk, *16% of autistic adults in the UK are in full-time employment*
[5] *Social Equality Commission and Gov.uk*, 2020
[6] *Twitter - Alyssa Milanos*

[7] Tallo, *Gen Z Demands Diversity and Inclusion Strategy,* 2020
[8] Boston Consulting Group - Rocío Lorenzo, Nicole Voigt, Miki Tsusaka, Matt Krentz, and Katie Abouzahr, *How Diverse Leadership Teams Boost Innovation*, 2018
[9] McKinsey - Dame Vivian Hunt, Lareina Yee, Sara Prince, Sundiatu Dixon-Fyle, *Delivering through diversity,* 2018
[10] *Median profit made by small and medium enterprises (SMEs) in the United Kingdom in 2022*, Statista
[11] *Harvard Implicit Association Tests*, 2018
[12] *Nuffield College,* 2019
[13] *Proceedings of the National Academy of Sciences,* 2012
[14] *Hewlett-Packard internal survey*
[15] Gaucher, Friesen and Kay, January 2011, *Journal of Personality and Social Psychology*
[16] *Gender Decoder*, Katmatfield, online
[17] Schmidt, FL & Hunter, JE, 1998, *'The validity of utility selection methods in personnel psychology: Practical and theoretical implications of 85 years of research findings'*, Psychological Bulletin.

7
Care

One winter's day early in my career, I found myself in tears in the office at 7.30 am: I'd arrived at roughly the same time each day that week to try and get ahead of my priorities and keep on top of things. My journey to work was on a particularly painful stretch of the M25, so I always left the house by six am to make sure I didn't sit in traffic for hours and rarely was there a day when I wasn't at my desk for ten to twelve hours. Clearly exhausted yet not quite realising this, I opened up my emails that day to find one which was particularly frustrating to me: I hadn't been given the pay rise I was hoping for and worse still, the business was hiring someone who I felt was doing an identical job as me for more money.

Now of course this wasn't the kind of upset which comes from a bereavement or the end of a relationship, but the kind of instinctive hurt I felt in that moment threatened to diminish everything I'd been working on for the past few months. I felt this was a very clear action that showed the business didn't give a toss about me. *Overreaction?* Maybe. But as soon as I processed the words on the screen, my tears started to flow. Not big sobs, but definite and distinctive tears that no matter how hard I tried to stop just kept coming. I've since learned that science supports the benefits this kind of 'leaking' makes happen and that it's needed to release the oxytocin and endorphins to make you feel better, but at the time, I was just so pissed off that I definitely wasn't thinking about the benefits it could bring! I just stayed in my chair and let them flow, all on my own.

Only it turned out that I wasn't on my own. Despite the fact I thought I had the office to myself, within minutes of me starting to cry, one of the directors of the business popped their head around the corner and sat down next to me. *(Did I mention that I was very junior in this company?)* There wasn't any need for them to ask if I was okay, as it was clear that I wasn't, but instead they just sat there with me at first. I'm sure that they may have experienced a smidgeon of embarrassment or confusion over what to do in this situation, but rather than scurry off, they very calmly acknowledged that I was upset and offered to talk it through and see if they could help. I can't actually remember what exact words they said to me, but I do know that within ten minutes, I'd gone from furiously upset to feeling calm and thankful. Calm because I really did feel better after having a good cry. Thankful that someone cared enough to show an interest in how I was feeling.

We've got your back

And whilst there are definitely many other times in my working life when I've felt supported, that was one of the first times I really 'felt' that someone had had my back. I felt happier and was able to discuss more rationally what options I had here and what the practical next steps were *(more sleep followed by negotiating my pay rise were the winners in this particular case...).* Whether that director realised it or not, in those few minutes, they'd not just helped me but helped their business as well.

Not just tea and Tampax

Everyone wants to feel cared for. And every company wants happy and healthy team members within their business. Stating this is how I start any training I do on health and well-being because it's the holy grail for any business, whether they realise it or not. Just being happy is not enough to create the MAGIC you are looking for: after all, you could have an office full of people who are happy but not achieving much. But being healthy as well puts everyone in a place to do their best. Health relies on caring: both for ourselves and others. And in the same way as we all want to do work which matters in order to show that we matter in the world, being cared for supports this purpose in life in making us feel more valued wherever we are.

Care in a work context is a broad church, of course, covering not just your team's health and physical well-being, but also their psychological well-being and how this plays out in your business: the culture and environment in which people work, how people treat each other in it and what this supports in terms of what work they do.

The entry-level understanding is what you are legally responsible for. However, when it comes to setting expectations with people around this section of someone's onboarding or management responsibilities, a cursory mention of the fire extinguishers and drills appeared historically to be what most people felt was needed in a typical office environment. For many years, our broader individual well-being just wasn't considered a factor in how ultimately successful people could be in their roles. And for the most part, this was something people were expected to take care of themselves.

In my experience, 'care' has traditionally also had a more 'female' energy associated with it. And as a young professional moving into the area of HR and People - coincidentally one of the few where women are the majority - I found quickly that in practice in many companies, it was also very much an area 'outsourced' to these teams. To some degree it makes sense of course, as HR and People teams have always had a watching brief on areas of well-being, but, *"Claire, I think I saw Sally going into the loo looking a bit upset. Can you go and have a word?"* was not an uncommon question to hear asked of me rather than be addressed by the person's manager. This perception of others being responsible for care and it being limited to when someone was upset is also possibly the reason why one of the more derogatory alternative team names for the

HR and People team I've heard in my time is *Tea and Tampax!*

It's not that in the past anyone asking this of me was a complete monster of course, but just that caring for people sat in an area of most people's minds which bordered on being way outside the remit of a day-to-day business and was often seen as best left to others. Or in some cases, sadly no-one at all.

Fast forward to 2023 and what a difference a couple of decades can make.

The evolution of work and what we know about the impact of well-being on business means that not only have I never heard that particular term since the late nineties, but that the area of care has evolved from something that can be solved by 'simply' having a cup of tea into instead being recognised as forming a major backbone in the HR and People strategy of any ambitious business.

Due in large part to the impact of caring for your team having a healthy, functioning and growing business being well documented, research from Gallup [1] also shows that it's easier to attract people into your business when you look after them, and easier to keep them there too. Well-being consistently shows up as a key area of engagement and 'stickiness' in employment. [2]

That's before we've even got to the fact that we need people on board and thriving to contribute as well.

All present and correct

Over the years, I've been taught to run numerous reports on sickness and absence rates as the main way of tracking well-being. I recall the national average number of sick days early on in my career was close to eight days per person per year and so we would congratulate ourselves if it was below five in any rolling period, as the inference was that this meant we had a healthy team. But whilst it might be one method of measuring impact to any business, it certainly doesn't tell the whole story. Absence is supposed to link to productivity: less absence equals more productivity. However, since 2000, even though our national absence rates have been declining until the last year or two and are one of the lowest rates in Europe (currently they're an average of 4.6 days off work [3] per year per person sickness in private companies versus seventeen in Germany, for example), we still lag behind the average productivity of all G7 nations when measured on an annual basis [4] *(and yes, Germany does come out ahead of us).*

So whilst there look to be technically more people 'present' at work than there may have been in the past, it's equally likely that there are other reasons for this which belie the picture of a healthy workforce it presents on paper. Two such reasons which may be offered for this are the need by some to 'look' present in their jobs and the need to avoid the financial challenges that come when their pay drops to Statutory Sick Pay *(currently c. £123 per week).*

There are many reasons why the health of your team has become a more significant factor in your own business success: overall awareness and discussion of these areas in public forums, productivity hiccups when people are off with health issues and where it has left a gaping chasm of skills, and knowledge when someone is absent, not to mention the dawning realisation that we couldn't continue working in the way we have been for many years.

I know from experience that well-being has featured heavily in the last couple of years in the kinds of issues I discuss with our clients. I also know that the issues it raises within the workplace can be extremely complex and often misunderstood.

But with attraction, retention and growth as key goals for most – *all of which are influenced by individual health* – it's time to get to know the different ways we can weave care into our business lives in a regular way.

Well-being comes in all shapes and sizes

At its heart, of course, it's built of simple principles *(isn't everything?)*. We know in ourselves that when we're happier we're more switched on and have more energy and so in turn, if your team's health is pukka, then you're more likely to experience greater engagement, a better quality of work and generally be working in a nicer environment.

Caring for others doesn't make us soft. It makes us human. It doesn't mean that we need to hug everyone we see who isn't smiling *(definitely not recommended in a work context, to be honest!)* and it doesn't mean that we need to avoid any conversations which might seem tricky if they're done with good intentions. But it does mean *metaphorically* putting your arms around someone, by understanding a bit more about their world and what you can do to support them, and by being clear about the things you see which they can do to help themselves.

When we feel cared for, we are more likely to feel positively about that person who has shown the care and for the overall experience and situation we are in. We are more likely to be honest and transparent about what might be impacting us, which in turn allows those around us (our managers, our colleagues) to be clear on what they can *(and sometimes can't)* do to help.

Health affects our wealth in all sorts of ways: our wealth of experiences and ultimately what we are capable of delivering and achieving. Unlike a general customer or product issue you may find in your business, the root causes of any issues related to our health are way more complex.

If you'd asked someone thirty years ago about their health, they'd have probably a) thought you rude for enquiring about something so personal or b) gone on to tell you how they'd got a dodgy knee or tennis elbow (or possibly both). This is because our attitude towards health has long been very centred on just the physical aspect of it without really much knowledge of, let alone consideration of, the other areas of well-being that all need to be kept reasonably in balance.

Typically speaking, there are *at least* six areas of our individual well-being you can help people balance as part of their overall health: physical, social, intellectual, workplace, mental and financial. And whilst it might not strike you that all of these things are things that you should *or even could* be concerned about showing care for when it comes to your team at work, each one of these has the potential to throw someone off balance and impact their success.

Let's get physical

Our physical well-being is typically first on anyone's agenda: *what we put into our bodies and what we do with them to make sure we are physically fit.* On the proactive side of things, businesses have realised for quite a while that if they invest in supporting people's physical well-being – *through subsidised gyms, yoga classes, fresh fruit perched in a bowl in the kitchen or (in the case of some more flush organisations!) free kombucha shots for those who return to the office* – then this helps boost their focus and productivity. Likewise, schemes such as the cycle to work scheme (a salary sacrifice scheme which allows employees to save money on bike purchases whilst encouraging a healthier lifestyle) have also been hugely popular since their introduction in 1999. And whilst we certainly can't control whether someone gets a life-changing illness, providing medical insurance to team members has long been one of the top five benefits provided by companies to support people if the worst happens.

Social harmony

Next up is social well-being and our need to have meaningful relationships. A lot of this goes hand in hand with Inclusion and our need to feel safe in our environments, something which can be shown at work by all those team events designed to get us creating and maintaining connections with each other. Picture if you will, the clamour to get on the various social committees created in companies. The free night out bowling or axe throwing is not just an excuse to have fun and *(given that we live in the UK)* have a few drinks too. Now, you can legitimately say that this is helping your well-being too!

Never before have we collectively experienced the impact of a decline in social well-being as we did in the year following March 2020 when we first heard the mandate, "You must stay at home." The impact on people of not being able to see their friends, families and loved ones for the months and months which followed this during COVID is just one of the factors which influenced an increase in people's anxiety, loneliness and depression. We'd never discussed social well-being as a real 'thing' before then or really made the connection to how a lack of it can hurt us, despite knowing that as humans we naturally need others to thrive.

Intellectual vitality

To a degree, our intellectual and workplace well-being go hand in hand with the chapters on Growth and Meaning and are concerned with how much we are being mentally challenged, how safe our workplace is physically and how much meaning we find in the work we do. And as we've already discussed in these two chapters, putting it bluntly, if we don't have strong workplace and intellectual health present in our lives, we are likely to get bored and either leave what we are doing (our jobs) or worse still for any business owner, stay physically but be mentally absent.

This, my friends, is where the term 'quiet quitting' comes from.

Financial flourish

Contrary to what many people think is the case, financial well-being is not about how big our salary is, but instead how we feel about our financial goals and the control we have over these. There's no need to delve into a team member's bank statement to pick it apart or even *(sadly for many!)* give them a rise to show care about someone's financial well-being, but instead, look at what support can be provided to help them improve it.

Setting aside a recommendation you pay salaries on a competitive basis, financial literacy is one area which any business can lean into reasonably easily and is an area which is lamentably under-taught and under-discussed at all stages of our life, despite it having such a significant impact on our overall well-being that it is the third most important reason why people skip work, as found by the Mental Health Foundation. [5]

During lockdown, in an attempt to understand how this area impacts employees as well as to increase my knowledge and application of it, I took a qualification in financial coaching. I didn't want to necessarily become a financial coach *per se*, but I knew that I would learn plenty from my peers and trainers and wanted to expand the various training sessions I already ran for my clients to include an awareness of financial wellbeing and its impact on employees' and their success. It was a steep learning curve for me. A lot of my peers were certified financial planners who knew the lay of the land a lot better than .! However, having successfully completed this qualification and delivered a number of sessions on this topic with people, it opened my eyes to how much more people can do in this area and encouraged many to work through their goals and challenges.

In my experience, individuals are much more likely to tell people about deeply personal aspects of their relationship history *(whether you ask or not!)* than share details of their financial health or challenges, such is the level of shame around our financial health. However, I was surprised and delighted in equal measure that by starting to talk about the fact that many have these challenges in these sessions, people felt safe enough to share their own experiences and how they worked through them. These ranged from one person who was once reduced to pilfering toilet paper from the office at the end of the month through to tales of uncontrollable credit card debt that was only reined in when the person was reaching their fifties. I can honestly say that during these sessions I've had some of the most eye-opening and frank discussions with any team that helped everyone involved.

Mental health

And finally - *last but by no means least* - there's our mental health. This area has probably had the biggest impact in UK professional work right now as shown by the numerous column inches, posts and issues that have surfaced in this area, something helped along considerably by the pandemic. Again, an area once reserved for hushed voices and stilted conversations, research from Mind shows that our attitudes towards mental health in particular have improved over the last ten years by some considerable margin [6] and it's now a very common area for discussion in any business.

We know that time taken to support and manage those with mental health issues is not limited to the individual who is suffering and the cost is also considerable: research by Oxford Economics estimated that mental health problems in the UK cost our GDP to the tune of £25 billion [7], something that will have only grown more prevalent over the last few years.

But even without these statistics, I'll bet that every single one of you can think of at least one of your team members or people you know at work who has experienced health issues recently - perhaps even yourself.

We at the HR hub team have seen first-hand the increasing toll that mental health issues have taken on business owners, leaders, teams and everyone (directly or indirectly) affected. The majority of businesses we work with have had at least one or two situations come up when their team's mental health had impacted them: from the major generalised anxiety people were feeling through to very specific acute conditions that someone was managing, the need for care has varied significantly.

Even before you unpick some of the areas relating to mental health and how you can support positive mental health in your team's lives and in your business, it's important to highlight that we all *have* mental health: good and bad. Given that most people typically refer to mental health in reference to the negative *(e.g. Claire is having mental health issues)*, I find it helps to think of it as we do our physical health: some days you might be a marathon runner, other days you might have trouble running to the door. And although there will be some people who have much more significant issues than the odd blip, it's never one hundred percent consistent in any of us.

Anxiety and mild depression come in at numbers one and two of the most common mental health conditions we have in the UK [8] and the good news is that most issues tend to be short-term: although work can exacerbate or even create issues in this regard, if the support is there in the right places there is no reason to assume there will be re-occurrences.

Like it or not, you have a big influence over your team's health and well-being. There are going to be some limits to the support and care that you can provide, of course;

however, there are lots of things you can do to show you care in this area that don't need to be expensive and don't need to be time suckers.

Hazard dodging 101

You might already know that a health and safety policy is one of only three compulsory policies that you need to have if you're employing people. It summarises who is responsible for what in your business, what you do to support people's health and makes sure you've assessed any risks to this on a regular basis. Legally, that is it.

And whilst there are reams and reams of information about your responsibilities you can find online *(and my small print here is that there are a lot of nuances and specific cases so don't rely on the following sentences as any defence)*, I can sum them up in a couple of lines: for most modern offices with good ventilation, regular fire checks and without people behaving irrationally, etc, the risks to the physical safety of your team will be pretty minimal. Your risks with the team's physiological safety, however *(which you are also responsible for whilst they are working for you)* are likely to be much higher.

This is because the biggest threat to people's health and safety at work in the past few years in most professional (and office based) workplaces lies with our mental health and not workplace accidents. If you work in a factory, of course, this is obviously not going to be the case - likewise, if you work with chemical equipment in a lab, etc. But I think you catch my drift that this piece is for those of you who have little experience in driving a forklift or donning a hard hat.

It is, therefore, your responsibility to assess the risks for your team when they're working for you (after all, you're the boss) and then decide what measures to put in place to protect them. I give you the dourly titled 'risk assessment', which should be updated and reviewed on an annual basis.

So whilst it is your responsibility in this regard, as I've mentioned before, your influence over someone's health and well-being at work is more than the physical elements put in place, as it relates to not just what you do in terms of formal documentation, but ***how*** you work together on a day-to-day basis.

Caring contractually

When someone joins your business, the contract we think of having in place is the one in writing, stored somewhere on our drive or HR system and which we rarely look at. Yet the most influential contract we have with our team members relates to one which is never in writing and only ever felt: the psychological contract. This unwritten set of expectations and obligations you both have covers things including perceived promises about their role, opportunities for development and how they are going to be treated whilst they work with you. This is built up over time. These day-to-day activities, from your tone of voice to your actions (inferred or otherwise) or even omissions, play a significant part in building up a culture where psychological safety is at play.

In the previous chapters I've mentioned the need for psychological safety to be present in any business in order to have a sense of inclusion and innovation, but these everyday positive actions of having clear communication, recognising and appreciating your team and respecting their opinions, all show a sense of care that builds on this. Consistency of action matters here and whatever you're regularly showing to your team – *care and respect, I hope!* – this is what they will come to expect as part of your psychological contract.

However 'unseen' it is, the contract can still be broken. Typically, this happens when you do something unexpected: getting 'shouty' at your team in front of others, ignoring people, not following up on promises made or changing your mind at short notice and with little or no consultation. Think of all the issues and resignations which happened when many companies 'ordered' their teams back to the office post-Covid: even though their place of work was technically and contractually the office for many, people had grown used to different expectations that (to them at least) had built up to contractual status. Although most issues were resolved without concern, when people start to mistrust your intentions or actions, it takes a while to rebuild these.

When it's the case that people don't feel safe, they will start to fear, not help you when they think there's a problem or just not speak up at all or blame others whenever they can to avoid being in the firing line. Conversely, if you show support by giving constructive feedback when a mistake is made, encouraging people to treat mistakes as learning experiences, listening to people when they speak and even - *very generally* - asking how they are, will yield the opposite.

Showing care, therefore, doesn't need to be complicated and reinforces a positive psychological contract: your tone of voice, for example, and the words you use in the workplace to talk about others, all influence this area in as many ways as the actions you take.

Health scares

If you're thinking, "Help! One of my team has just told me they have concerns about their mental health; what do I do?" Relax - that's nearly one in six people you're talking about at some point, so if it's the first time you've heard it, it won't be the last!

Caring for others is not an area you need to be frightened of and you are certainly not expected to be an expert in this area *(either by law or by your team)*. What is expected, however, is that you listen and research to understand what is going on in each situation and that you always try to be 'reasonable'.

It's true that being reasonable is a fundamental principle in our employment law landscape, but it's also a fundamental principle we should all look to adopt in daily life. If your team member comes to you saying that they're a bit stressed and anxious, is it going to be reasonable that you fire them? No, of course not. *Is it reasonable that you ask them what their concerns are and see whether it is some-*

thing you can do anything about? Yes, of course. In many cases, there may be issues that don't even relate to work which affect your team and that you can't change. But if you can't change their personal situation, you can change how you respond to them and the care that you show towards them. It will be remembered.

Surveys can sometimes help you identify common causes impacting your team if it is work-related and you can ask your team directly to share what support they need. However, there is a wealth of support out there for when things get more complex or when you feel your knowledge or your time has reached its limits.

One client of ours uses their online system *(Notion, in this case)* to extensively showcase a range of information to raise awareness of health and well-being issues and in the past has used a Time to Talk day to encourage team members to share their own (mostly anonymous) experiences of health concerns to de-stigmatise things. As a result, they find that their absence rates are quite low for the industry and where there are challenges or someone has a concern, people feel supported by it rather than rallied to leave the business.

Or you can always call in others.

An employee assistance programme (EAP) is a low-cost way of providing support to your team too. The schemes – which evolved from insurance provisions designed to mitigate and pre-empt any health issues which issued potential claims – typically include a 24*7 support line for all employees to be able to call anonymously to speak to a trained counsellor. As mentioned earlier in this chapter, they recognise that the types of support needed and areas will vary considerably and so people can call up on a range of issues from relationship issues, drink and drugs through to financial ones. They're very easy to set up and, when used and promoted in the right way, very helpful.

Drinking your own (apple cider) medicine

As with almost every other area in this book which helps create the magic in your team, you need to also include yourself in this equation too. If you don't look after yourself and show self-care, then it's likely the impact will be greater than on anyone else on your team having issues combined. Self-care, therefore, is the number one thing you can do to show you care about your team, as well as yourself.

Running a business can be extremely tough on the mind and body of anyone and the burnout risks are high. In the early stages, it's not uncommon to see business owners pack up as the impact on their health - their relationships, physical health, etc. - becomes too much. And often we notice the signs that something needs to change later than anyone else. One of the most common signs I've observed of acute stress in business owners is an inability to make decisions. It's not that they tend to shout more or are shorter in their conversations (although maybe that happens too in some cases), but such is the volume of decision-making needed each hour of every day in many businesses, that it can become too much for many.

Self-care is not a thing restricted to face packs and scented candles or filling your body with apple cider vinegar. All these things can be great healthy habits of course, as can getting to know your own triggers, release valves and practising those too. And whilst we may often undertake big energetic bursts to focus on – *marathons, triathlons, cycling races* – sometimes some genuine, consistent, positive self-talk can do the trick too.

Your Action:

1. Keep an eye on your absence data and reinforce your expectations over working patterns so people aren't just 'present' in a physical sense.
2. Choose a few areas of well-being in which you feel you can support and share resources to help people.
3. Create a culture of psychological safety by listening to how people are feeling, either one-to-one or through surveys, and treating them with respect.
4. Take time to uncover what someone may need when it comes to their own health support: every individual is different and so what works for one person may not be the same as the next.
5. Practice self-care on a regular basis.

---

[1] Ben Wigert, Gallup, 2022, *The Top Six things that people want in their next job*
[2] Best Companies Research from Best Companies has consistently shown that Well-being is a factor which influences an individual's engagement with any business.
[3] Safeworkers, 2022, *Average Sick Days Per Year*
[4] ONS, 2020, *Comparison of Productivity Measures*
[5] Mental Health Foundation, 2023, *The Cost of Diagnosed Mental Health Conditions*
[6] Mind.org.uk, 2014, *Greatest Improvement in Public Attitude to Mental Health in 20 years*
[7] Oxford Economics, 2016, *The economic importance of safeguarding mental health in the workplace*
[8] Nice, 2011, *Common mental health problems: identification and pathways to care*

8
In Conclusion: It Can't Make the Tea

And now we come to a close. Thank you for reading this far. My hope is that the contents of this book will not just have given you food for thought but also the inspiration to take action with your own team.

After all, the concepts introduced through the MAGIC framework are not about complex strategies or convoluted policies. They are about nurturing Meaning, being clear about Accountability, encouraging Growth, cultivating Inclusion, and prioritising Care, all things which you can do without being an HR or People expert or investing heavily in time or money.

You can use the framework to check in on your current plans, to find opportunities to boost what you're doing already, or to resolve issues where you see there's a gap.

It can provide solid foundations for your culture as you grow: no need to keep asking, "How do we do things around here?" as the answer will be obvious to everyone working with you.

What do solid foundations give, of course? An excellent base to grow! Accelerating your plans becomes easier and with less 'noise' along the way.

And last - but by no means least - for all those having difficulty hiring (that's everyone in 2023, by the way...) having a great framework in place can also help showcase you as an employer they want to work with. Whilst even the best employers get an occasional bum Glassdoor review, the ones with consistently poor scores are there for a reason!

Unfortunately, however, the MAGIC framework can't help you with everything.

It definitely can't make the tea. But it also can't cater for every eventuality you come across. *(Come on, your team aren't robots!)*

So yes, there will be things that arise during any team member's lifecycle with you that are not in 'the plan' that cause a bit of angst and a bit of challenge. Even in the most positive environment, multiple characters will find a way to have a few little niggles from time to time.

However, being authentic about what your intent is, and having solid foundations and good practices to back these up will make sure that you're in the best place possible to manage any hiccups along the way.

Good luck!

Acknowledgments

I've had the real pleasure to work with & know some truly lovely people over the years that have influenced many of the practices I've adopted and shared in this book: clients, colleagues and friends alike. And some who are all three.

To become an expert in any area you need the chance (and support) to be able to learn through successes and failures, something my two favourite managers - Jon and Petrina - both gave me by the bucketload. You also need a solid HR-crew to bend an ear, shoot the breeze and be there for those *"they did what?!"* moments: Rosie, Hannah, Amy, Nicola, Milly. You are all ace.

You're not in the HR-world, Kate, but I feel you are an honorary member of this particular society too. There isn't much on 'people stuff' we haven't covered over the years on our morning calls and so if you ever get bored of the hospitality industry, just say the word!

Great teams come from great clients & I truly am lucky to have some amazing ones. However, particularly thanks to those who've stayed the course across many years & put your faith in me - Nick, David, Sarah, Mark, Patrick, Tom, Ben, Will, Joy - remember, no problem is too obscure!

Thank you to Sarah for the clear (& frank :-) feedback on earlier drafts of this book. And to Bridget, Mum, Molly & Alison for your continuous support. To Penny and Lucas for their encouragement in making me believe I could do this and of course to Owen for the title!

And last but definitely not least. Thank you Kenton, Billy and Digby for feeding me cups of tea, leaving me alone to stare at the wall until I started to write and letting me hog whichever room I feel is my 'writing' one that day.

About the Author

Claire Ward has over twenty-five years of experience in the People and HR space, working with many award-winning and fast-growing businesses to solve their challenges. Working both in-house and consulting, Claire's expertise stretches from small-scale start-ups to global employers.

In 2015 she founded The HR Hub (www.thehrhub.co.uk), a leading HR outsourcing business helping hundreds of UK SMEs to hire, manage and grow their teams.

Claire lives in Kent with her family.

Printed in Great Britain
by Amazon

39818057R00089